GARDEN DESIGN SOLUTIONS

Stephen Woodhams

GARDEN DESIGN SOLUTIONS

IDEAS FOR OUTDOOR SPACES

jacqui
small

For Mum and Dad, who supported and encouraged me into the world of horticulture, and also – with thanks – for my sister Stephanie, Peter Parsons, Ian Rees and John Bateson.

First published in 2015 by Jacqui Small LLP
74–77 White Lion Street
London N1 9PF

Publisher Jacqui Small
Senior Commissioning Editor Eszter Karpati
Managing Editor Emma Heyworth-Dunn
Senior Project Editor Zia Mattocks
Art Direction and Design Manisha Patel
Production Maeve Healy

ISBN: 978 1 910254 02 8
A catalogue record for this book
is available from the British Library.

2017 2016 2015
10 9 8 7 6 5 4 3 2 1

Printed in China

This basement-level outdoor room (page 1) acts as an outside dining room, with a self-circulating zinc water feature and a living wall on either side of it. This makes a very calm and restful place to sit on cream upholstered Louis XVI-style armchairs with a Perspex coffee table, which is functional but doesn't interrupt the view. The cream clay pots planted with standard olive trees (*Olea europaea*) are underplanted seasonally, here with *Helleborus*.
The Cotswold gravel pathway with a galvanized metal edging (page 2) zigzags like a Greek key design through the planting of *Helichrysum italicum, Santolina chamaecyparissus, Teucrium fruticans* and a square panel of *Ophiopogon planiscapus* 'Nigrescens', among which, one year, I planted white tulips. Galvanized pots of tulips also migrate through the garden.
These overscaled white pots (right) are in a row of five. The central one has a gloss finish and is planted with a standard olive tree, while the rest have a matt finish and are planted with West Himalayan birch (*Betula utilis* var. *jacquemontii*) and *Eucalyptus gunnii*.

CONTENTS

INTRODUCTION

Garden Design Solutions has given me a lovely opportunity to share with a wider audience the communication and language of the design of gardens, using the materials available to us these days as well as new flower varieties and plants. However small or large your plot may be, once finished, if it takes you on a journey without you having to go anywhere except to wander around within its perimeters, it's working. It should help you to relax and hopefully change your mood as it uplifts and gently elevates your spirits, allowing you to unwind and appreciate the natural beauty that plants bring to a garden.

Some of my favourite ideas are shown within the following chapters. I have been most fortunate to be able to design many gardens around the world – from England and the Mediterranean to Dubai, Barbados and Mauritius – and this book has given me a great opportunity to revisit gardens that I have so loved being involved with. It has also given me the chance to share the details of some garden designs and the solutions I created to meet the different challenges that each garden presented, as no two gardens are ever the same.

Every garden should be about individual expression and passion, and one's unique interpretation of a space. I try as often as possible to put my clients' visions into this interpretation, as then they will hopefully feel a sense of ownership and be more interested in helping to develop and look after the garden I have created for them. To this day, I am so very grateful that I am still passionate about creating gardens for other people to enjoy for the rest of their lives. I truly believe that spiritual comfort and peace can be achieved by nurturing plants within a garden. I am convinced that experimentation is the best form of self-expression and our wellbeing often depends upon it. I hope this book will help you to evaluate your own outdoor space, with such issues of privacy and use, and will inspire you with solutions and ideas to enable you to create a unique and relaxing garden.

This seating area (opposite top left), bordered with *Agave attenuata* and a hedge of *Elaeagnus* x *ebbingei*, is lit by strips of sunlight shining in between the fabric panels covering the pergola. The grey leaves of the *Cotyledon undulata* on the Cotswold stone block work well with the grey velvet exterior fabric. **The glass balustrade (opposite top right)** reflects the self-contained zinc water feature and allows a view of the three galvanized pots of seasonal tulips. **The stone walls and steps (opposite bottom left)** make a beautiful backdrop for the old *Olea europaea*, with the mounds of the *Santolina chamaecyparissus* and drifts of *Agave americana* and lavender. **Alternate chocolate and cream clay pots (opposite bottom right)** planted with assorted sempervivums require minimum maintenance, and I adore the mix of colours.

PLANNING &
DESIGNING

GETTING STARTED

Analysing the existing outside space that you have to work with and identifying your priorities in terms of how you want the garden to work for you and everyone who will be using it is the first stage of any project.

When planning your garden, it's always useful to look first at the surrounding landscape for inspiration. In a country garden you may be able to blur the boundaries and borrow views from the countryside around you. This is something that many great landscape designers do; historically, designers such as William Kent in the early part of the eighteenth century used this principle, often punching holes through boundaries to the views beyond. Obviously this isn't so easy – or in many cases desirable – in an urban environment, as you are governed by the existing boundaries that are generally shared. So here you may need to draw inspiration from the surrounding architecture or trees – what is often referred to as the 'borrowed landscape', the glimpses of the area that surrounds the particular site that you want to develop or change.

The two enormous trees (left) were the reason we constructed this raised deck at the back of the garden – their bases were so huge and the ground already sloped up to them, so it made sense to keep the existing level. We designed central timber decking steps leading up to the seating area and we set the decking boards within a frame, with a central ethanol fireplace and a pair of matching sofas facing each other to keep it all very symmetrical.

Planning the layout of this terrace carefully (above) was vital to make sure everything fitted and still left enough space for the items to breathe and not look too cluttered. The result is the most lovely outside drawing room, especially when the canvas blind (shade) is drawn out on a hot, sunny day. The overscaled pots around the perimeter give a lovely backdrop to the whole space.

We dressed the front of this Mediterranean building (previous spread) to make more of an arrival zone and to create a sense of welcome. The pair of Italian cypress (*Cupressus sempervirens* Stricta Group) add emphasis to the arched windows, while the three clay pots planted with *Agave americana* create a central feature.

Many of the materials that you might end up using to build your garden would have come, at one time or another, from the landscape around it, so that is often the best source of inspiration. Bear in mind that a garden doesn't always need a large number of plants. Often you are able to rely on what's around you, and it is the details that you may decide to add to dress or furnish a space that give you the context for the garden.

Whether you enclose a space and how you choose to do so can fundamentally alter or define the character of a garden (see page 86). This decision leads you on to the next very important factor: the form the garden will take – its shape, its layout, its spaces and how they interrelate, their proportions and uses.

In the country gardens we design, I think it's always important to try to get the garden to blend seamlessly with the surroundings, as I think we achieved here (opposite) with the *Cupressus* and *Olea europaea*. On roof terraces I always try to frame a view if it's worth having, as we did with the London Eye (above), but sometimes you need to screen the outlook. This is an important decision to make early on in the design process. This particular roof terrace (below) has a great view out to sea, but we needed to screen the neighbouring roof, which also helped to enclose the space, making it a really lovely, sheltered suntrap.

IRRIGATION

An important aspect to consider early on in any garden project is irrigation, which naturally plays a very important role within most gardens. Depending on where in the world the garden is located, it may be prudent to try to use plants that can cope with drier situations or ones that may need irrigation only to get themselves established; often, the more water you give a plant, the shallower its root system develops and it will become dependent on a watering system. We try to use plants that are native to a particular landscape if they work with the design we are wanting to create. For instance, when putting together a Mediterranean garden, I like to use succulents and cactuses, which are often drought resistant.

Many of the built-in irrigation systems we install are water-harvesting systems, which collect rainwater and use it for irrigation. Rainwater is often much better for the plants than what I call 'town water'. On some projects we use recycled grey water for irrigation, which adds to the 'green' credentials of a property.

I always like to try to create gardens that are a further series of rooms extending from the house, with the garden as a bridge between the house and its surroundings. Creating distinct but linked spaces within a garden makes the whole space seem larger.

Invariably, I find that the most successful gardens have a distinctive atmosphere, and the creation of the atmosphere should be a key consideration for anyone designing a new garden. To some extent, the mood of the garden may dictate the way in which it is used. For example, you may wish to create a garden that will encourage contemplation, so you should ensure that each element of the design is sympathetic to this aim. You may decide to plant aromatic species along a pathway so they release their fragrance when brushed against; engaging all the senses – sight, sound, touch, smell and taste – does make a wonderful atmosphere in a garden. This is why, in my RHS Chelsea Flower Show garden in 2002, 'The Sensory Garden' sponsored by Merrill Lynch (see also page 160), I used Stephen Cox's *Five Senses* sculptures along one wall.

In 'The Sensory Garden' (above), designed for the Chelsea Flower Show in 2002, Stephen Cox's grey granite sculptures representing the five senses look wonderful against the white rendered boundary wall. The lovely planting outside this house (opposite) dresses the otherwise sterile space and makes it feel welcoming, while providing a cool haven to sit in the shade on a hot, sunny day.

When you first see a site, whether a new build or an existing garden, it's your initial impression – that instinctive and often strong feeling when you first see something – that should guide you in your further thoughts about its design. I truly believe that you should follow your instincts, as when I haven't done so, I have been disappointed with the results.

There are a few basic principles you need to establish. Which way does the garden face? You may like to have an eating area where, in the summer, you might choose to eat breakfast, for example, but it will be no good if that spot in the garden doesn't get any sun until late in the afternoon, perhaps due to the shadow of surrounding buildings or trees. It takes time to fully understand all the characteristics of a garden, so I like to spend some time within a space to really soak it up. If you have the luxury of seeing the site at different times of the day, that can be very useful in helping you decide where to place what.

I also have to consider my clients' ideas and understand their needs and aspirations. I like to try to incorporate their ideas into their gardens, as it gives them a sense of ownership of the design. It always helps to prioritize, too, when thinking about what budget there is to spend on the garden.

It's very helpful to write a 'wish list' of what things you might like to see within the space, as a garden is always a result of a series of questions and decisions. These details are very important because they give the garden a sense of place and convey how it will be experienced. How the different elements are put together and how they connect with each other form a narrative that gives the whole space a meaning and purpose. Every garden should have a coherent narrative, for a garden that is disjointed is a garden that doesn't function. Furthermore, a list of what you might like to do within the space, such as grow fruit and vegetables, entertain friends, cook or just contemplate and relax, are all very important layers to be considered as well.

Creating and putting together a garden design involves adding different layers – definition, form, detail and planting – all of which will interact with each other

We were asked to update this typical 1970s-style garden (left) in line with the property's redesigned interior, as well as give it a more practical means of access.

and together create the character of the garden. Planting (see also page 148) is one of the most important layers, and the selection of plants is key. Many of my ideas are based on using plants to add structure, especially evergreens, which create a pleasing effect during the winter, and often plants are chosen to connect with the surrounding landscape. My favourite layer of all is seasonality. It is great to use a tree for its structural identity, and if it happens to flower and have great autumn colour, then it ticks several boxes at once. Colour is also a lovely layer to add, as it can completely change your mood and alter the concept of a garden and the feeling created within it. Nature cannot, and should not, be excluded from even the most modernist of garden designs; a garden is as much about self-expression as it can be about imitating natural effects. There is always a link between nature, culture and cultivation.

When demolishing an existing garden, do look at what things can be salvaged and reused, such as the power supply for exterior lighting, or materials such as old paving or brickwork, which could be used for new hard landscaping. It's always good to recycle where you can.

ASK YOURSELF SUCH QUESTIONS AS:

- What activities do you want to be able to do in the garden? For example, grow your own fruit and veg, cook, eat, entertain or just relax.

- Do you need to include a children's play area? If so, does this need to be near the house, where you can keep an eye on things, or screened off in some way?

- Do you need to incorporate storage?

- Would you like a water feature?

- What style should the garden be?

- Do you have any favourite plants you would like to include. If so, are they suitable for your garden's aspect and soil type?

- What do you want to put into it and, very importantly, what should you leave out?

The 3-D artist's impression (left) shows how we wanted the garden to look. We designed four zones: the first being the entry to the garden; the second its new staircase from the basement level; the third the cut stone terrace with its inlay of timber decking to represent a rug for the dining table to sit on; and the fourth the raised timber deck with its exterior fireplace. The pleached trees give privacy as well as balancing out the height of the timber pergola, over which we planned to grow climbers to provide a natural canopy.

The completed garden (right) shows the top of the stairs (zone 2), leading to the dining area (zone 3) and the raised deck (zone 4), with its exterior sofas, coffee tables and umbrella, as the client decided not to build the pergola at this time. The 'Big Idea' of zone 2 is to allow the yew (*Taxus baccata*) hedging to grow through the metal railings over time so that it appears to be just a green hedge, but with the added safety to stop anybody falling down to the basement level (see also page 78).

CASE STUDY
THE MULTIPURPOSE GARDEN

Originally created by a property developer, this simple outside space on three different levels wasn't working for the new owners, and we were engaged to turn it into a multipurpose garden that could be used by all the family. The interior designer, Joanna Wood, together with the client, had chosen a Mediterranean look to be used throughout the house. We needed to inject some style into the garden design and, working closely with Joanna, we continued the Mediterranean theme.

The aim was to create a versatile garden that functioned well as a whole but that also provided distinct areas for different activities on each level, to cater for the various needs of the family.

The basement of the house originally comprised an open-plan kitchen and dining area, and then a series of sofas leading towards sliding doors into the garden. We wanted to create a larger outside space on the same level as the interior, so that the sliding doors could be opened onto an exterior dining area. To achieve this, we first had to excavate and take out a series of terraced built-in planters. Having reclaimed the floor area, we placed a central zinc water feature along the retaining wall as a focal point, with a living wall on either side of it so that we kept plenty of soft foliage in view from the windows.

In the centre of the large expanse of wall shared with the neighbouring property, we placed an almost double-height mirror edged in timber, the same as we had used

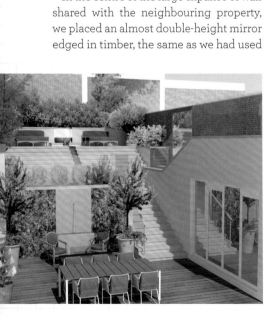

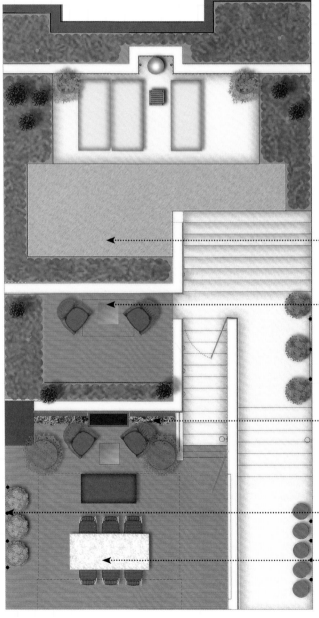

First, we worked out the four zones as a sketch and drew them up as a 2-D flat plan in conjunction with our wish list. Then we looked at the plants we wanted to use and the heights they may reach, so we could produce a 3-D view of the garden. This helps understand the space and how it may look once planted.

Faux lawn in front of a lounging area.

The chairs and coffee table can be moved to reveal the sandpit, which is covered to protect it from animals when not in use.

Living walls on either side of the zinc self-contained water feature make a green backdrop for the seating area.

One of two wall-mounted mirrors.

Marble-topped table to match the kitchen worktop inside.

The plan (opposite right) shows the as-built design; you will see in the 3-D drawing (opposite left) that we had proposed a central rill of water, but the client wanted a lawn area for the children, hence the redesign, which softened the whole look of the top part of the garden.

As this is a family garden (right) we had to introduce gates for safety, and these were made of glass to match the balustrade and keep an uninterrupted view of the garden wherever you are standing. Excavating down deep can be a costly exercise, but to make the basement more user-friendly and let more light into the interior, it was well worth the expense and effort. We completely replanted the garden, including the rear flowerbed, as I wanted to add some good evergreen structure. We did this by planting a lovely pair of multistemmed *Osmanthus fragrans* and *Agave americana*, as the colour of these works so well with the *Olea europaea* and the other plants with silver and grey foliage.

for the decking to keep the palette of materials simple. The mirror was aligned with the middle of the dining room table. This was a bespoke piece, with a marble top designed to match the worktops in the kitchen and so enhance the connection between inside and outside. The mirror makes the space feel much bigger than it really is. We also created a lovely seating area in front of the water feature – the perfect place to have a morning coffee or read the newspaper.

The middle level of the garden provides an alternative casual seating area, which can also be used for drinks before dinner. To make the space really multipurpose, a section of the timber decking lifts up to reveal a children's sandpit. In an urban space such as this, it's always a good idea to be able to cover a sandpit, as this not only prevents rubbish from getting into the sand, but it also frees up the space for other uses, such as a party.

The upper level of the garden provides a place for the adults to sunbathe and chill out while the children play on the artificial lawn in front of them. There are now so many good faux-grass products on the market, and if I hadn't said it was artificial, you would never have realized that it wasn't real. The large overhanging tree in the neighbouring garden meant that real grass would have struggled to grow well in this location, so artificial grass is the

perfect choice, as well as being reasonably low-maintenance and cost-effective.

In order to have uninterrupted views of the garden but still keep it a safe place for the children to play in, we used glass panels to create balustrades on each level, as well as glass gates that could be locked for further safety. This gives each level of the garden an almost Damien Hirst-type quality, where each section looks as if it's contained within a glass cube or tank, and makes each plant behind the glass balustrade look like a botanical specimen. In keeping with the transparent barriers, the egg sculpture positioned centrally behind the upper level terrace was placed on top of a clear acrylic plinth, which gives a surreal feeling to the space.

To give the garden the desired, strong Mediterranean identity, we introduced lovely vertical *Cupressus* trees, together with various styles of olive trees and multistemmed *Osmanthus*, clipped *Buxus sempervirens*, clusters of *Iris germanica*, lavenders and white agapanthus.

To echo the chosen theme, we used Louis XVI-style dining chairs and armchairs upholstered in an exterior fabric that co-ordinated with the fabrics used in the interior. Five old-fashioned French zinc laundry tubs were planted with seasonal plantings to introduce a splash of colour. Within the rest of the garden we used cream clay containers that are a very similar colour to the existing stone steps that we had retained.

The glass balustrades that surround the level above the basement (above left) make the sections of the garden behind them seem like botanical plantings within large glass tanks. They open up the space, while still providing safety at all the level changes.
Wherever you sit in the lower dining area (above right), there is a great view due to the mirror reflecting the entire space.
The child-friendly first level (left) can be completely enclosed with a glass gate and a section of decking lifted up to reveal the children's sandpit.
The zinc water wall (opposite) was placed as a central feature with living walls on either side, together with a Perspex coffee table and two upholstered Louis XVI-style armchairs. The sound of water, together with the dappled sunlight under standard olive trees, adds to the sense of calm in this sunken oasis.

LAYOUT

Once you have decided what areas you would like to include in your garden – such as a place for lounging, a dining space and a visual walkway with seasonal planting to connect them – you need to decide where best to position them.

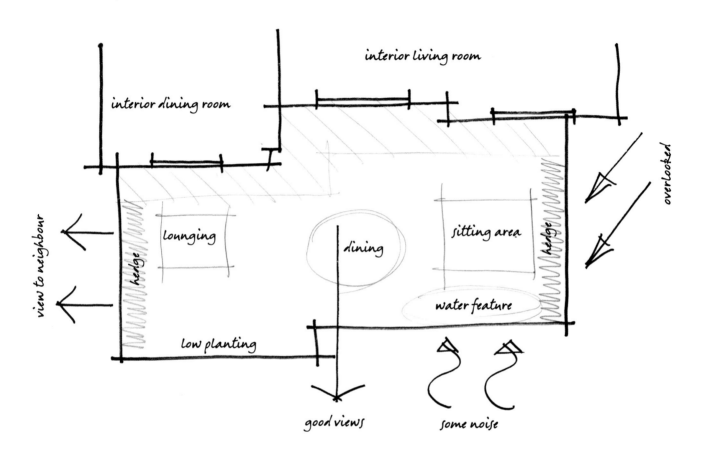

interior living room

interior dining room

overlooked

view to neighbour

hedge

lounging

dining

sitting area

hedge

water feature

low planting

good views

some noise

The key things to consider are how these different areas will relate to each other, to the interior of your home and to the surrounding landscape – whether that is a stunning view over rolling countryside or water, or the fact that one end of your plot is overlooked by your neighbours. You also need to take into account the aspect and path of the sun, and any shade created by surrounding buildings or trees.

Before you start planning your garden in detail, it is important to have properly surveyed your site and to have accurate measurements of it, as the base plan is always your starting-off point. You may get a plan from the estate agent (Realtor) or a previous owner, but double-check its accuracy; in particular, do spot checks to

establish that any existing key features and underground services are where they are supposed to be, as this could save you a lot of money in the long run. In the case of a large garden, or one with different levels to deal with, it's often better to employ a qualified surveyor to measure it up and supply you with an accurate digital plan.

Do look out at the garden from all the windows of a property, at both eye level and from above, and imagine the views you will see from them, as this can inform the rhythm and shapes you use outside. For example, if you are looking through long, rectangular windows, you could create a series of rectangular beds to reflect this – make the beds symmetrical

if they are to be a pair or stick to odd numbers if there are more than two. Sometimes in a rectangular plot it can be interesting and amusing to have diagonal paths allowing you to cross from one side to another. The introduction of water gives a garden an additional dimension, and a series of pools can help you deal with any changes of level within a space as well as form an interesting feature.

Think about practicalities, too. When you are deciding where to position a dining table, it is obviously sensible to try to site it near to your interior kitchen, so you don't have to walk too far with the hot food. You could also have your barbecue area adjacent to the table for ease of cooking and serving.

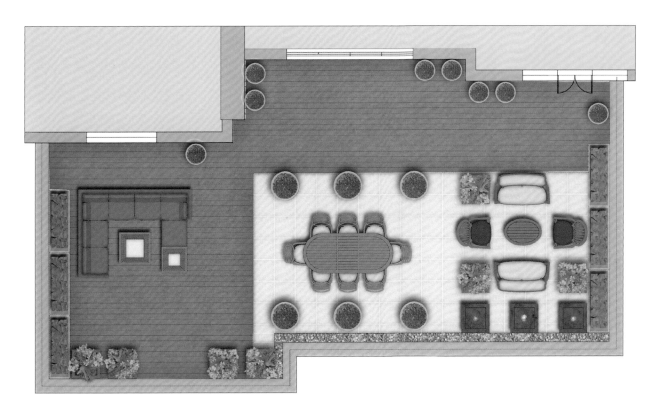

Always begin with a simple sketch (opposite) to highlight any issues that need to be considered from the start, at the same time as you are thinking about how the space might be divided up into different zones for various uses. The next stage is to draw up a flat, 2-D plan (above). This shows the zones for dining and formal seating on the stone surface on the right, and the more relaxed end of the roof terrace on the decked area on the left, furnished with a large double-ended L-shaped sofa for sunbathing on. The 3-D view (below) gives an impression of how the finished design will look, with the balanced arrangement of box (*Buxus sempervirens*) spheres in clay pots and a row of large containers planted with pleached hornbeams (*Carpinus betulus*) and yew (*Taxus baccata*) hedging, which makes a lovely suntrap to relax within.

This is a great view (top) across all three zones of the roof terrace, towards the end planter with its three tall, pleached hornbeams, underplanted with yew hedging. This provides a screen from the neighbouring roof terrace, as well as connecting the space to the surrounding landscape and making it appear larger than it is. The straight-sided, cream, clay pots (above), planted with overscaled box spheres, are positioned like an avenue, with the dining table placed centrally. This gives the terrace a majestic feel all year round.

When designing this rear garden (below), we constantly had in mind the family who were going to be using it. We split the space into four different zones to cater to the various requirements of all the family. The first zone is the main terrace of York stone with brick detailing, together with flat-pruned plane trees (*Platanus* x *hispanica*) to give the feeling of a contained room under a natural canopy. To the left of the garden, behind the existing garage, we placed a formal fruit and vegetable garden, within hedges of *Buxus sempervirens*, and a crisscross of paths leading to the working part of the garden, with its storage shed and compost bins. The third zone was the area laid out to lawn with shrub boundary borders, leading you on to the fourth zone at the end of the garden. This was more of a woodland-type area, complete with children's climbing frames, swings and a Wendy house, together with a rear access to the woods beyond.

We were asked to show, by means of artist's impressions, alternative versions of how the garden would look using different design ideas. The first option (above) shows the garden without the large, flat-pruned trees, but with a central, circular dining table and a rectangular canvas umbrella to provide a shady spot for lunch.

The second version (above), shows the terrace with four flat-pruned trees planted in each corner, together with a timber pergola for growing climbers, such as white-flowering wisterias with their great hanging panicles, which would fill the air with their subtle fragrance as well as providing natural shade.

Another consideration (above) was to put a swimming pond into the lawn behind the terrace, which would work well with the woodland behind, as it was conceived to be a very naturalistic style of pool to complement the rest of the garden.

CHANGES OF LEVEL

This was a lovely garden where, once again, we were able to work hand in hand from an early stage with the interior designer, Susie Beart. We followed the client's brief to maximize the space and accentuate the feeling of a link from the interior to the outside. We also needed to have a series of level changes, so that when in the basement of this property, you didn't feel that you were down in a big hole.

Our biggest hurdle was to provide privacy and screening to both side boundaries. The bottom of the garden was already secluded by a garage building and a low wall, but on one side was a neighbour with direct views onto the garden and on the other a road with traffic noise that we wanted to try to reduce. We decided to plant matching pleached hornbeams on both sides, with the trunks of the trees opposite each other. On the neighbour's boundary we also wanted to excavate as close as we could to maximize the size of the lower space. This wall was then planted along the top with ivy, which cascaded down over it to create a green wall. Quite soft in appearance, it also helped to form a connection with the upper, main part of the garden.

The lower garden was divided into two by a pair of shallow steps, incorporating a central planter, leading up from the dining space to a relaxed seating area in front of a central red glass water wall. Water runs from a pool in the upper garden along a central rill and cascades down the glass before being recirculated to the top pool. We used red glass to match the kitchen worktops and splashbacks (backsplashes), which are in the same red glass. This was the accent colour we took from inside to out, so we chose the lovely red-leaved and red-flowering *Lobelia cardinalis* 'Queen Victoria', together with a red-purple-leaved *Heuchera villosa* 'Palace Purple'. Large timber containers planted with evergreen standard trees, often underplanted with red seasonal flowering plants, underlined the theme.

Because this was a relatively large space, I changed my rule of practice and ran the timber boards from front to back.

We placed an interesting piece of sculpture in the centre of the originating pool of water, which catches the sunlight really well.

The seating area in front of the water wall is very restful. A glass balustrade ensures a link between all of the spaces, making the garden feel larger than it is.

Normally, I wouldn't have laid the deck boards in this format, but we were reusing the framework of the old decking, so boards had to be laid in accordance with the existing joists.

We decided to use timber Oxford-style planters to echo the timber deck.

I usually advise that timber decking should run from left to right as you look out onto it from the house, as that will make any garden space appear larger than it really is, but here that wasn't an issue. As we were also using the timber decking to clad the steps and sides of the lower area, it looked stronger laying it in this direction.

The clients decided not to have our regulation glass fitted along the edge of the upper level where the rill meets the top of the water wall (above left), as they felt quite safe and wanted to keep an open feel to the space. The central red glass water wall (above centre) with matching pairs of containers on either side creates a great vista. The black furniture acts as an interesting contrast within the space. The main steps (above right) that lead from the lower level up to the garden gate are also clad in timber, with a clear glass balustrade. The central planter incorporated into the shallow timber-clad steps on the lower level (below) breaks up the large expanse of decking and helps divide the space into two.

The back wall of this water feature (right) is made from a sheet of red glass, down which the water cascades before being recirculated to a pool above via a UV filter that keeps it crystal-clear. The kitchen that opens out onto this space features red glass splashbacks (backsplashes) – using the same material in the garden establishes a strong link between the inside and outside. The wall of glass acts as a stunning backdrop to the clay pots planted with *Kalanchoe luciae.* The central tree, *Tetrapanax papyrifer* (opposite), provides a good canopy of shade during the summer months. I love its bold, architectural identity with the soft, seasonal underplanting of red petunias and *Helichrysum petiolare.*

CREATING A THEME

Whether you are creating a garden from scratch – such as for a new-build property – or undertaking the renovation of an existing garden and home, it is often appropriate to base the design around a colour scheme or design theme that echoes the interior.

When you bring in a colour scheme as an idea around which to base your garden design, this could be a thread of colour taken from the interior and woven through the garden, connecting the two spaces together. For example, if you have an interior wall in a particular colour, you could then paint just one wall outside in the same colour, blurring the divisions between indoors and outside. Using coloured walls within a garden adds to the sense of containment and enclosure, which helps to create a sense of safety and protection for you and for the plants. I very much like architectural statements such as these, which should be very pure in form and accentuate either the vertical or horizontal dimension of a garden space. Which colour works better for a statement wall depends on where the garden is in the world. I like to use bright colours in sunny countries but am wary of using them in the UK, as they can often appear dull and out of character, unless they are used as an element of surprise, on the reverse of each wall, for example. I find that grey, taupe and earth tones look good everywhere, as they enhance the colour of the plants. Blue and hot pink work well as a backdrop for architectural-looking plants, such as cactuses, as well as flowering forms.

At one London property (see right), we had the inside and outside of the house painted in the same shade of cream, the interior flooring and the outside terrace were both the same cream limestone, and the freestanding walls in the garden were painted cream. The reverse of the walls, however, were painted bright orange, which provided a great visual link with the orange sideboard and bright orange floor cushions indoors. This also meant that any seasonal colour we added to the garden, such as tulips and hyacinths in the spring, were always orange varieties, planted in lines to echo the walls.

It is important to think about the colour scheme you are creating with regard to every aspect of the design. When we were thinking about gravel pathways for this particular project, we had to use Cotswold chippings, as these were a perfect colour match to the cream limestone of the terrace. The pathways were edged with galvanized metal to link with the metal containers that were used throughout the garden scheme. It's ideal to have two or three complementary colours to work with as part of your palette. The second colour we used here was lime-green, and there are a lot of plants that have attractive foliage in the perfect shade of green, especially the flowering lime-green *Helleborus foetidus*, *Euphorbia characias* subsp. *wulfenii* and *Alchemilla mollis*, as well as structural trees, such as the flame-shaped hornbeam when it first comes into leaf. The third colour we introduced was black, in the form of horizontal lines inside

The view looking across the Perspex and glass table (above) towards the black granite exterior worktop, where we placed two glass cylinders filled with water and flowers, lit from beneath. A glass canopy at the second-floor level offers some protection from the rain. **The reverse of the floating arches and walls (opposite)** are painted bright orange, which complements the central water wall and provides a great backdrop for the plants. The planting as a whole adds a soft layer to the garden, but the shape and texture of the plants themselves are bold and dramatic.

the house – the kitchen worktops and fireplace shelf – and parallel lines of planting in the garden – such as *Viola* Aero Series, *Helleborus niger* and *Ophiopogon planiscapus*.

Another way I like to bring colour into a garden is to take a dominant colour or material used in a room that opens onto the garden and echo it within the garden. We did this in a house designed by Susie Beart (see pages 26–9), where the red glass of the kitchen worktop and splashback (backsplash) was used as part of a water feature to form a wall down which the water could run from a rill on the level above into a reservoir, before being circulated back up to a pool at the top. We also introduced plants with red foliage and flowers into this garden, including *Lobelia cardinalis* and red *Impatiens* and the lovely red-edged *Kalanchoe luciae*.

This terrace (above left) is a great example of a scheme that was defined by the colour of the surrounding buildings. The umbrella fabric was chosen to co-ordinate with the strong blue façade, and the silver-grey shades of the architectural-looking plants also work well with this base colour. **We were unable to plant into the ground** in this area covered in gravel (above right), so we decided to place a series of different-sized square containers in a random design and plant each one with a single variety of plant to make bold, simple statements. **This blue painted window (below left)** was the everyday colour used on all the windows of this house, and we dressed them with agaves in cream clay containers to give interest to both the inside and outside of the property. When we hosted a wedding at the property, I suggested we painted the windows pink (below right) to tie in with the theme – a simple gesture that makes all the difference. I like them both for different reasons.

The scatter cushions on the white sofa and armchairs provide the only splash of colour in this outdoor seating and dining area (top and above), with its simple timber flooring. They are blue and white during the day, for a fresh, bright vibe, but are changed over to red and white versions during the late afternoon to give a completely different feel. These take on a great look under the setting sun and make the space feel warmer as the evening draws in. Once again, a simple yet effective idea.

The design of a garden may also be influenced by the interior identity or theme. A roof garden we created had an African theme (see left), instigated by the interior designed by Joanna Wood. We came up with a timber-decked floor with inset panels of three types of wood, which gave a zebra effect. The metal powder-coated containers placed around the perimeter were alternate cream and chocolate to emulate an animal stripe, and these were planted with spiky, colourful plants, such as varieties of *Phormium* and *Astelia* and ornamental grasses, to give a tropical, jungle-like feel.

The sculpture was inspired by an original African tribesman shield; we commissioned it as three shields, set within pebbles and uplit with copper light fittings to tie in with the colour theme. The water feature was modelled on assorted African vases I had seen, and we took various shapes and produced them as silhouettes, made of torn strips of lead, set within a still pool of water. The trough of large-leaved bamboos made a perfect backdrop, and as they moved in the wind, the rustling sound gave another dimension to the space. To echo the theme further, we designed a zinc-covered table to link with the lead sculpture. The two high-backed chairs at each end of the table are reminiscent of Zulu throne chairs, with lovely, weathered wooden benches on either side that add an organic, earthy feel. This terrace also had low clay planters, alternating once more in cream and chocolate, planted with low sempervivums to look like desert-style planting. Detail is always important when creating a theme, so here we placed galvanized square planters on the table, planted with *Kalanchoe luciae*, the beautiful red edges of which linked back to the colour of the fabrics used within the interior.

Three panels of herringbone-design wood (far left) set within the deck of this roof terrace create three different zones, giving the illusion of more space.
Cream clay containers (top left) were planted with different varieties of *Sempervivum*, which are fairly drought-resistant and low-maintenance, so do well in exposed areas such as on a roof terrace.
These *Kalanchoe luciae* (centre left), with their lovely bold leaves, are one of my favourite succulents. The square galvanized planters – a series of three always works well down the middle of a long table – sit well on the zinc-clad surface.
The square planters (left), in alternate chocolate and cream, reminiscent of animal stripes, are planted with phormiums and grasses that grow well on rooftops, to conjure up the mood of the African Bush.

GATHERING INSPIRATION

Inspiration for design can come from many different sources – it may be something as abstract as the colours or shapes in a work of art or a natural landscape. As part of the design process, I often like to put together a mood board as a collection of ideas, to go with the design concept.

I like to draw inspiration from the past, as I believe that is how we learn and adapt existing ideas in order to create new, contemporary designs. I always make a mental note about anything interesting I've observed on buildings or in gardens and landscapes while I'm travelling. I often note how plants grow in a large, natural landscape, as this can influence my choices on a smaller scale – for the style of plantings within a flowerbed, for instance. I also tear pictures out of magazines and newspapers, as well as creating a Pinterest board on-line.

When I put together a mood board for a design concept, this might include objects, swatches of interior and exterior fabrics, and samples of possible materials to be used for the flooring, fences and even the type of mulch, as this helps to set the feel and context for what we are trying to inspire.

This open-plan room (above right), which looked out onto a roof space, consisted of a kitchen, dining space and living area. I was able to design both the interior and exterior of the property, so when putting the materials together to create the mood boards, I was considering both spaces at the same time and the ways in which they would relate to each other.

I wanted to keep to a tranquil palette of grey, white and turquoise, so we chose grey porcelain tiles for the floors, inside and out, and white Carrara marble for the interior and exterior tabletops. I also used this marble for the worktops, to upgrade the standard kitchen, and added a mirrored splashback (backsplash) that reflects the garden and so makes the apartment look much bigger. The timber slatted seating outside will weather to a soft grey; the sofas are topped with grey canvas scatter cushions, while the Louis XVI-style armchairs are upholstered in

grey exterior velvet. We also selected other exterior fabrics in turquoise, cream and grey. Poles of silver birch were used to make plinths, the base of the coffee table and the fireplace. Olive and eucalyptus trees were planted in keeping with the colour theme. I favour the less-is-more approach and often find that working with a tight palette of materials results in a stronger effect.

The starting point for a mood board may be anything from an artwork or object to a colour, material or plant. In this case (opposite), stems of natural cotton appear in a photographic artwork that we wanted to use within the room that opens onto the roof terrace, so they gave us the starting point for selecting the textures and colours for the mood board. The next task was to decide what applications each item may take in order to build up the completed garden.

GET ORGANIZED

It is important to plan everything down to the last detail – from structural elements, such as surfaces and materials, and water or other built-in features, to the colour and style of the planting and containers, to the furniture and accessories. Not only must everything work together visually, but orders and deliveries also need to be scheduled so that everything arrives on site at the correct time. We often present a client with a three-dimensional visual showing the proposed design in detail, including new levels and types of materials to be used as well as a suggestion of the planting style and ideas for furniture.

The mood board (opposite) that we put together for this house and garden (this page and pages 30–1) was built up from a base palette of cream – cream-painted rendered walls, cream limestone for the flooring, with cream Cotswold chippings for texture and mulch, and cream fabrics for both inside and out. We then introduced three accent colours: black for the kitchen worktops and fireplace hearth, and for some plants; orange for the reverse of the statement wall outside and in flowering seasonal plants such as tulips, as well as for lacquered surfaces, fabrics and flowers inside the house; and lime-green, within the planting and lawn, but also in vases and chargers for decorating the table. Clear glass walls and balustrades, together with Perspex furniture, gave a seamless link between the interior and the garden.

Cream limestone was used both inside and out (left), and in the living space that looks onto the garden we also used a cream wool-coir rug edged in black webbing to echo the black rubber sofa and lead the eye out to the garden.

Looking back though the garden towards the house (below left), a blockwork, rendered wall, painted bright orange on the reverse only, frames the path of Cotswold chippings lined by galvanized containers that echo the grey metal window frames. They are planted with orange and burgundy tulips for spring colour.

Pairs of tall, overscaled cream clay pots (below), planted with seasonal colour, flank the doorway on the limestone entrance apron, set within the granite driveway setts. These lead the eye right through the house and into the rear garden, with the central water wall at the end of the vista. The black edging on the rug echoes the metal door frames and emphasizes the straight lines within the design.

LINKING INSIDE & OUT

As part of the design process, I always look into easy and clever ways to link the inside space to the garden outside and vice versa. Creating a coherent style or colour theme between the interior and exterior results in a calmer space, where nothing jars. It also makes both the garden and the room inside seem larger than they are, as the transition between the two becomes seamless, making it feel like one large space.

One of the easiest ways to achieve this link is to use the same or similar flooring materials both inside and out. For example, a natural stone may be honed for the interior and flamed or rough-sawn for the exterior; or a grey, limed-wood interior floor may be chosen to match the colour of timber decking outside when it has weathered to a silver-grey over time. Travertine and limestone can work well in this application, as can porcelain or grey concrete paving slabs. The same idea can apply to your choice of materials for other surfaces, too, keeping to a limited palette throughout the design – the same stone for a kitchen worktop as for a dining table or coffee table in both the house and garden, for instance. This principle can also apply to seating and even fabrics, as there are now some wonderful exterior-grade velvets, linens and chenilles available.

The 4m- (13ft-) wide, double-height glass doors (below) give a view right through the property to the tall clay pots on each side of the front door, on the limestone entrance apron. As all the walls are painted in the same colour, you are never sure whether you are inside or out.

The vista continues from the back of the house to the Ben Nicholson-inspired water wall at the end of the garden (opposite).

This entrance area (right) is graced with overscaled pots planted with *Brahea* palms, underplanted with *Syngonium*, which connect with the larger palms outside. Placing tall, white, faux *Agapanthus* plants on the central table, together with a collection of ornamental decorative vases, makes the garden seem to flow right through the covered space and links all the areas together. **We used the same flooring throughout the entire ground floor (below) and** placed exterior furniture inside, so once again you are never sure whether you are inside or outside. By placing the cream clay containers planted with frangipani (*Plumeria*) trees against each upright, we softened the whole frame of the building, and the lovely fragrance drifted right through the house.

Another clever way to link the inside of the house with the garden is to paint all the interior and exterior walls in the same colour, so you are never quite sure whether you are inside the house or out in the garden. Alternatively, paint just one exterior wall, which may be a boundary wall, and take the same colour onto one feature wall inside.

We tend to go to a lot of trouble to link a colour through several items in a garden. For instance, the fabric used for the sofa cushions may match the canvas blind (shade) over the seating area; an umbrella and the metal containers in the same space may be colour-matched. Such co-ordination strengthens the story and makes it look considered, but still retains a simplicity.

I also like to work within the same tonal colour. In a basement walkway (see below), we painted the interior walls white like the exterior walls, making a pleasing backdrop for textured cream clay pots. The pots, planted with tree ferns, are on metal frames with wheels, so they can be moved around easily for maintenance.

This dramatic basement light well (above left) has three glass sides, looking onto a wooden bench with a living wall behind it. The trickling from the zinc water feature breathes life into the subterranean rooms. **In this conservatory (above right),** with its natural rendered wall and concrete paving, you could be outside. The chocolate-coloured clay containers were chosen to match the leather tub chairs and dark stained-wood coffee table. **For this bedroom light well (below),** we wanted something with an architectural identity that would tolerate lower light levels, so we chose *Dicksonia antarctica* underplanted with a circle of *Asplenium scolopendrium.*

CASE STUDY
DISSOLVING WALLS

This was a great project for our design office to be involved with, as we were able to work hand in hand with an architect and direct the style of the extension that was being added to this property. We wanted to create a galley kitchen in what was originally the side access path to the rear garden, and we also added a glass box onto the back of the property, which is the main seating area. It is a lovely space, as even when it is raining you have the sense of being outdoors, yet are cosy and warm inside.

I wanted the back of the property to feel as though it were floating on water, so we created a wraparound pool, with a small filtration unit to keep the water crystal-clear. The entrance to the garden is via three concrete stepping stones (odd numbers always look more architectural). I wanted to find an inexpensive type of stone flooring that could work both inside and out and give the space a slightly industrial feel. The solution was concrete paving slabs.

The industrial feel was emphasized by large concrete rings that are usually used as drainage collectors in the construction of motorways. These were stacked on top of each other to create tall, 125cm- (4ft-) diameter containers, which were planted with *Fagus sylvatica* (Atropurpurea Group) 'Purpurea Pendula' and underplanted with seasonal planting. A circle of neon lighting in either hot pink or purple was placed around the base of each concrete ring to echo the colour theme, and the table and chairs were painted in the same colours.

We also always co-ordinate the exterior flowering plants with the interior. The pink and purple *Impatiens* that provide summer colour work really well with the pink and purple LePage sculptured vases on the radiator shelf, and the green of the *Buxus sempervirens* co-ordinates well with the green rug.

Our designs are always about the detail. Here we had the frame of the glass box and all the other glazing finished in a dark grey metal, and we linked this with three tall square planters made from zinc, which patinates beautifully (see opposite top). They were planted with *Buxus* ball topiary and placed in a line within the pool

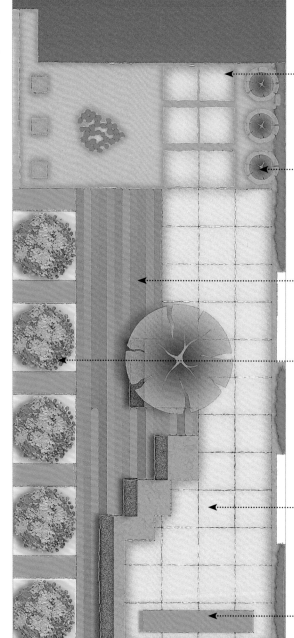

Grey paving stones continue as stepping stones through the shallow L-shaped pool.

Three tall brown clay containers planted with box (*Buxus*) balls.

Softwood timber decking painted grey.

Concrete drainage rings planted with weeping purple beech – *Fagus sylvatica* (Atropurpurea Group) 'Purpurea Pendula' – and underplanted with seasonal colour.

Grey paving stones, as used for pavements.

A slatted timber bench with views towards the house.

Looking into the glass extension across the pebble-lined pool of water (above), the green rug looks like a panel of grass, creating an interesting play on the idea of a lawn inside the house. The eye is drawn along the decking (left) towards the conservatory by the row of oversized containers and the boards themselves, here laid from front to back. *Echeveria* growing out of weep holes in the concrete rings add a quirky touch. The small garden easily accommodates a colour-themed dining area for six to eight. The specially dyed orange canvas umbrella provides shade over the pink slatted table and purple chairs, which tie in with the alliums in the concrete rings.

of water. Opposite are three tall circular containers of chocolate-brown clay, also planted with *Buxus* ball topiary. The colour of the clay is echoed inside the house by the leather armchairs and the wenge wood of the dining table and built-in storage units.

The planting of structural evergreen hedges of yew (*Taxus baccata*) and panels of *Ceanothus*, a blue-flowering evergreen, was planned around an existing *Sorbus* tree that happens to bear amazing orange fruits, and we used a great orange-flowering *Canna* 'Phasion', which is also very architectural in its leaf form and strong vivid flowers.

The bright orange umbrella (opposite) links well with the *Canna* 'Phasion', which I love growing as much for its flowers as for its foliage. **We implemented everything from our original mood board (left).** I particularly like the spot fabric, used as runners over the back of the dining chairs, as it features all the accent colours used inside and out. The dark brown mulch for the flowerbeds is a perfect colour match for the built-in wooden units and leather tub chairs.
We took the legs off the coffee table (below) and placed it on the rug to give the space a Zen-like quality. Cat-grass growing in a clear glass container and hot-pink and orange roses make perfect decorations.

DESIGNING & PLANNING LIGHTING

Lighting and irrigation (see page 14) are practicalities that need to be thought out in detail at the planning stage of your garden project, as it's important to ensure that the infrastructure is set up before the underfoot surfaces are laid and the planting is in place.

Whatever size of garden you are designing, lighting plays a very important role and will enable you to conjure up a mood that can be dramatic and theatrical, even if the budget allows only a few lights. Well-thought-out lighting can make all the difference to a garden design and I consider it as important a factor as the choice of construction materials used for the hard landscaping and the combination of plants.

Lighting technology is advancing very quickly these days, as are the types of fittings available. It is a good idea to use a lighting designer on even the smallest of projects – as specialists in their field, they should be very up to date on what is available and so will be able to advise you on the most cutting-edge fittings. You need to be very careful not to overdo the lighting within a small space, but some of the LED (light-emitting diodes) and fibre-optic fittings that are now available allow more flexibility and are generally getting smaller and more discreet. These can be used to create subtle uplighting, spot lighting, and wall and floor washes, and can be set within various types of flooring surfaces or directly within the ground to light up specimen trees.

One of the key roles of lighting is to help create a depth of field within a garden space, as nothing is worse than looking out from inside the house at night-time into a big, black hole. Lighting can create some magical effects, and I like nothing better than being able to see the rain, wind or snow in a garden at night; it makes the space feel like part of the interior.

The dominant lighting effect on this roof garden (right) is the LED colour-changing lights that we inserted into the underside of the rim of these large, white, plastic pots bordering the terrace. The colour can be changed according to mood or occasion, and the white takes on the colour of the light, shown here in green. With the additional effect of uplights through the trees, the lighting is mainly on the perimeter of this small garden.

LIGHTING KNOW-HOW

Large and small spike-mounted spotlights Available in various sizes and colours, directional spike spots are perfect for uplighting trees or specimen plants.

Paving-recessed uplights These can be used in driveways, paths, terraces and decks, or placed between pots to highlight them or create interesting shadows.

Wall-recessed lights for steps We often place these on every other or every third step within a flight for safety.

Submersible lights for water tanks Placing lights within water creates a magical effect, not only lighting falling water but casting shadows through it.

Sometimes what you don't light in a garden is just as important because the aim is to evoke an atmosphere at night, which can easily be lost by having too many lights. I particularly dislike floodlights, as they make a garden feel flat and uninviting. Lighting should be all about creating a sense of mystery and surprise, almost like moonlight or candlelight, and by this I mean defining what I call hot and cold areas within a garden. This can be achieved by having focused light, such as a spotlight on a specific feature – a statue, tree or shrub with good winter structure or coloured stems – and softer, diffused light, such as candles on the table.

Lighting has the power to instantly change the mood or tempo of a garden space. For example, a roof terrace can be easily transformed into a calm and sensual space at night by lighting it only with exterior nightlights and candles in storm lanterns, together with an ethanol or log-burning fire-pit to keep the chill away. This creates the perfect, restful mood for chatting and admiring the stars, especially in rural areas where there is little light pollution. I always take this into account when advising clients on how much lighting to use in a country garden.

Illuminating a water feature at night adds another dimension to the space. A water wall, which I often use in my garden designs, can be lit to create magical effects. The frosted- or coloured-glass panel down which water cascades can be backlit, so when the water falls into the reservoir at its base, amazing shadows and reflections are thrown against the wall and through the water.

Take into consideration how much ambient light may come into the garden from the rooms that look onto it. On this decked area (right), light comes up from the basement below, so we focused the fittings around the perimeter of the garden; the light reflects in the mirrors opposite in a magical way. The only lights we had on the lower terrace were spotlights directed onto the trunk of the old olive tree in the clay pot and onto the centre of the table. On the upper level, uplighting the trunks of the tree ferns creates lovely shadows against the rear red brick wall and brings a 3-D quality to the trellis columns.

Spike spots lighting the stems of pleached magnolias (far left) also send lovely shadows up through the squares of trellis.
In this modern garden (left) two recessed lights were placed centrally within timber steps (out of view) to send a wash of light over the panels of white gravel. Spike spots light the front and rear pair of spiral yew and cloud-pruned trees underplanted with spring bulbs, and the two side panels of bamboo. The water feature is lit by submersible lights behind the frosted glass.

Subtle lighting is always a good choice for a dining area (above left), being more romantic and restful. Here the LED strip light under the built-in bench gives the space a lovely, warm glow. Blue neon light, set under frosted glass within a metal channel (above centre), gives a real wow factor to this black slate terrace, edged with white pebbles for a dramatic contrast. Wall-recessed step lights (above right) cast an ambient glow into the lower courtyard and, together with the two up-down wall lights on the side trellis wall, they give ample light to this minimal outside space. The raised square planter in this seating area (below) has a magical, floating quality due to the LED strip light built into a shadow gap on the underside. The three uplights highlighting the trunks of the flat-pruned *Platanus x hispanica* trees also create a great effect on the underside of the leaves and make a sculptural feature of the bare branches in the winter.

Taking advantage of reflective surfaces in your garden, such as water, glass and mirror, can enhance the magical effect of your lighting design. For example, LED strip lights can be installed at the base of a glass balustrade, so the light travels up through the glass and illuminates the edge. The effect is of a clean line of light carving up the garden.

Certain ways of lighting can create mystery or add a bit of drama to the garden. For instance, edging a simple, black slate terrace with a blue neon strip light, safely enclosed in a metal channel topped by a frosted-glass panel, makes the space hum like a spaceship and creates something truly magical to look at, especially from a distance. For a similar but more ambient effect, a line of light can be added around the lower section of a raised planter. During the day, this looks like an ordinary shadow gap, but at night a simple LED strip mounted inside the gap gives a clean, contemporary line of light all the way around the base of the planter, so it appears to be almost floating within the space.

Uplighters are extremely versatile tools that can be used in different ways to create theatrical effects. We often set recessed uplighters within decking or paving; positioning them in between containers creates great shadows. I also use them to subtly light posts on either side of a driveway. Recessed lights can also be inset into vertical planes – walls or steps – to wash the floor with light. This helps to give a greater feeling of depth to the space. Uplighters can also be placed within containers to uplight the plants. This works especially well with sculptural shapes, such as evergreen topiary. I love to uplight mature stems of trees, the wooden uprights of a pergola and even umbrellas around a pool. When flat-pruned trees such as *Platanus* x *hispanica* are in full leaf, the light is reflected beautifully on the underside of the leafy canopy, creating a lovely dappled effect.

If you have a garden on two or more levels, consider using fewer light fittings in the lower section to make it a softer, moodier place in which to relax, perhaps with only a pin-spot directed onto the dining table to highlight some container planting in its centre.

In certain locations you cannot beat candlelight. On this roof terrace (previous spread) exterior nightlights, storm lanterns and a log-burning fire-pit make this outdoor lounge space a great place to relax and enjoy the sunset. On an environmental level, it also pays to be conscious about light pollution in rural locations. Placing deck lights in between these square clay pots (above left) creates a pleasing pattern of shadows playing across their surface. This white plastic pot (below left) is lit by two types of lighting. The first is the colour-changing LED, shown here in purple, which casts the glow of its colour onto the white surface (see also pages 48–9). There are also two spike spots that light up the multistemmed *Betula utilis* var. *jacquemontii*, which looks great at all times of the year, but especially in the autumn when its leaves turn a wonderful shade of golden brown.

CASE STUDY
PERFECTLY LIT

We took a soft approach when we came to design the lighting for this garden, as we wanted the space at night to appear to be lit by candles; but we were also mindful that there are several level changes within the garden, so the lighting of the steps was an important factor. We placed recessed lights at intervals in the walls on one side of the staircases, so they washed light along the treads of the steps and, by default, gave a great wall wash to the lovely red brick walls that surround the garden, resulting in a space with a real sense of warmth.

The nature of the planting in this garden is that it has very strong vertical elements, achieved mostly by the tall *Cupressus* but also because of the two fine specimens of multistemmed *Osmanthus*. Uplighters were positioned to highlight the multistemmed nature of these trees, as well as to uplight the stems of the standard olive trees planted in pots on the lower level. As the garden was to have a Mediterranean theme (see also page 18), we chose some lovely French-style wall lanterns with a copper finish.

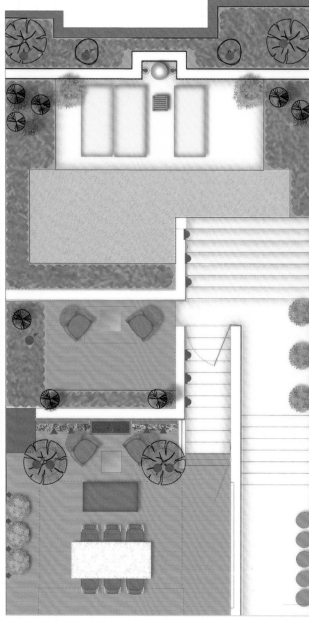

Large and small spike-mounted spotlights

Paving-recessed uplights

Wall-recessed lights for steps

Submersible lights for water tanks

Recessed step lights (above) were set into the left-hand wall to light every other step with a soft, ambient glow; the secret is to ensure the light sources can't be seen from the house. **The overall effect (opposite)** of the combination of step lights, uplights and decorative wall lanterns is soft and warm.

SCALE &
PROPORTION

BALANCE & SYMMETRY

Creating a sense of balance, whether by playing with size and scale, shape and form, repetition or textural contrast – or sometimes a combination of all of these elements – helps to create pace and interest within a design.

The starting point is to have a really good look around a site at the planning stage and decide on what the 'Big Idea' might be. The springboard for this is often an existing feature, such as an established tree, a surface that you don't want to change, a vista that you would like to make the most of or an entrance that you want to make more imposing. At one Mediterranean property we worked on, the front courtyard already featured two majestic and tall *Phoenix dactylifera* palms, which gave the entrance a great wow factor. We thought these needed to be connected to a more human scale, even if still a bit overscaled for the space,

Creating balance is one of the most important factors when designing any garden space. In this garden (left) the central water feature, inspired by the work of abstract painter Ben Nicholson, is balanced by the two floating, blockwork, rendered walls on either side of it. This arrangement is emphasized by the pair of galvanized pots of *Tulipa* 'Orange Emperor', with one placed on each side of the timber-slatted bench in front of the water wall.
Pairs of the same clay pots, planted with the same species of cycads (above and previous spread), together with pairs of orange trees in beds edged with low, green hedges, beautifully dress the entrance to this house, mixing their formal, architectural style with the loose habit of the trees.

This square plot (left) is totally paved, except for narrow side beds, where espalier pears grow on the walls, and a wider flowerbed at the back, edged in *Buxus sempervirens* and with a central, seasonally-filled urn on a plinth. The height of the boundary wall is extended with panels of painted diamond-style trellis supported on posts in the ground. In each corner of the courtyard are oversized, square, zinc containers, planted with standard olive trees underplanted with silver-grey foliage plants and white-flowering herbaceous plants.

so we decided to place a pair of very large rimmed pots outside the courtyard walls, planted with majestic cycads. I love the architectural quality of these palms, which require only pebbles at their bases, as loose underplanting would lessen their bold impact. We placed another pair of similar overscaled pots part of the way along the pathway, almost centrally within the space, planted with a further pair of mature cycads with textural, aged trunks; these formed a sort of avenue, taking your eye right up to the front door and thus creating a magnificent entrance. This was the 'Big Idea' for this space and it proved to be very simple yet very effective, as the pairs of cycads are quite the opposite to the rest of the planting within the courtyard, where there are orange trees, with their informal and loose habit, together with irises for the spring and roses for early summer flowers and fragrance.

Another way to create balance is to use similar, if not the same, materials in different ways within a garden; in a small space, this can sometimes create a magical effect. In a compact city garden, we positioned four square zinc planters, 1 x 1m (3 x 3ft), on each corner of a raised terrace (see above), planted with clear-stemmed olive trees and loose flowering underplanting, such as iris, white agapanthus, lavenders and *Helichrysum*. In the centre of the lower terrace, we placed a self-contained zinc water feature, 50cm (20in) tall and 80 x 80cm (32 x 32in), with pairs of seating in the form of Lloyd Loom chairs on either side. The repetition of the zinc surfaces helps to create a connection between the two different areas.

This water feature (opposite) had to be practical as well as interesting to look at, as the first pathway is the main entrance to the property, with the water flowing over the wall between the two pools. I always prefer to work in odd numbers, so we designed each pathway through the water to be three large stepping stones, which look like sculptures within the water. The tiles lining the pools are the same as the ones we used in the main swimming pool. I love how the tall, matching cypress trees are reflected in the water.

I positioned these tall, skinny pots, planted with evergreen box spheres (above), to create a sense of balance in the view up the stairs from the main house to the roof terrace. The front two pots emphasize the double-width space, as the stairs themselves are only half the width. I used the corner pot against the louvred fence as an anchor for another pot further along, making another pair, further echoed by the pair of stems of the pleached hornbeams in the distance. The glass balustrade ensures nothing hinders the view.

CREATING IMPACT

Whatever size of outside space you have, creating an impact will give your garden a real presence and sense of style. It is possible to do this in even the smallest of gardens or courtyards, often by repetition of the same or similar types of container, by unexpected changes in scale, or by the use of an unusual or oversized object that adds instant drama. If a bold, statement colour, a contrast in texture or a theatrical lighting effect is thrown into the mix, the end result will have even more punch.

One of the most effective ways to create impact is by repetition of the same object or container, and this has become one of our signature ideas. I often use a pair of identical oversized pots to flank an entrance, thereby making it instantly more imposing. I also like to use the idea of placing a series of identical containers in a row, sometimes leading the eye down a set of steps and often following the line of a boundary wall. This allows you to introduce some greenery into a space, at whatever height you wish, in areas where it is not possible to plant in the ground, such as on a roof terrace or in a small front garden. If there are tall trees the other side of the boundary in a neighbour's plot that could serve as a backdrop, choose plants or trees of an intermediate height with appropriate underplanting to complement the 'borrowed landscape'. Using pots and planters that tone well with the other materials and colours in your garden always creates a cohesive story, while unusual containers make a strong statement. For extra impact, select your planting to tie in with accent colours used elsewhere in the garden and inside the house.

Using plants in pots like individual sculptures, or in this case like an art installation down a long staircase (right), can be a very effective way to provide visual interest. The cactuses require minimal water, so here they are also a practical solution, as it would have been difficult to install an automatic irrigation system in this location.

I love finding quirky and interesting shapes of trees for our designs, as they always add a special layer to any project. These lovely old olive trees (opposite) make an unexpected contrast with the clean, modern, architectural backdrop, and add a sense of history and authenticity to this newly built garden.

Overscaled pots (above left) can make you smile when planted with something unexpected, such as this line of 1m- (3ft-) tall, white terrazzo pots planted with tall, clear-stemmed *Magnolia grandiflora*, underplanted with seasonal colour in the form of orange winter pansies. **This impressive wooden front door (above right)** needed something dramatic to soften its appearance yet keep it bold and inviting, so we planted a pair of standard *Olea europaea* with two circles of grey-leaved *Echeveria secunda* var. *glauca*. The large, cream clay pots echo the colour of the stone, and their thick rims reflect the outer edge of the arch. **I wanted to soften the boundary wall** alongside this clean-lined, mirror-edged swimming pool (below left), so I placed a simple line of five large, cream clay containers, planted with beautiful *Bismarckia nobilis*, which are a lovely steel-blue colour that often echoes the colour of the sky and surrounding water. These are underplanted with *Aechmea fasciata* 'Primera' x 'Morgana', which has grey-blue foliage to match the palms and brilliant-pink, cone-shaped flowers. **These imposing containers (below right)** were made from a stack of Milton concrete rings (normally used for underground drainage), rendered and painted chocolate-brown. They are planted with 5m- (16ft-) tall *Phyllostachys nigra* that look amazing when uplit at night.

I often use this method of placing three identical pots in a row (left). These cream clay containers planted with spheres of *Buxus sempervirens* look simple but effective in this modern front garden with its panels of Cotswold chippings set into a stone frame. The row of taller, skinnier pots along the boundary creates a change of pace.

I love the industrial identity of these Milton drainage rings (below), stacked up to make impressive containers and placed close together to maximize their impact. Planted with weeping *Fagus sylvatica* Atropurpurea Group and underplanted with pink and purple *Impatiens*, with *Echeveria secunda* var. *glauca* growing out of the weep holes, they look magical with the circular rings of neon light around their bases.

INCREASING A SENSE OF SPACE

I always like to make a space feel bigger than it really is. This can be achieved in many ways, but my favourite is to stagger hedges, topiary or pleached evergreens through a design, similar to a theatre set where you have a proscenium arch and layers of scenery that jut in and out of view, and a focal point of the main backdrop at the end. I try to use this trick wherever possible. Pathways and lawns can also be narrowed at the end to create a false sense of distance.

Mirrors and other reflective surfaces, such as a black glass tabletop or water, can be used within gardens to create some magical effects. They can also make small spaces feel a lot bigger than they really are, as well as making them seem more interesting by reflecting the surroundings and sky. Sometimes it's possible to hang mirrors within frames of the same style or material as the existing windows, which unifies the space at the same time as reflecting it. A well-placed mirror can enable you to see more of a garden and give you two of everything reflected in it, so the greenery seems more lush and opulent as a result. It is also possible to achieve some great effects after dark with night-time lighting reflected in a mirror. Sometimes I use mirrors to break up a line of fencing. In a small garden, a useful trick is to insert a mirror into a boundary wall to reflect the internal space, in the same way as in a larger garden you might break out a section of an inner wall, of either rendered blockwork or a growing hedge, to expose a view or vista. The mirror creates a similar effect with an interesting dimension, as if you have more space than you really do.

I also like to add 'floating' walls to give further interest to a space (see opposite top), and the division in both height and width often makes a space feel bigger. This can also be implemented with plants in the form of hedges planted at angles, or by using different fencing materials, trellis (see pages 94–5) or metal. Sheet metal can be laser-cut to any design and then powder-coated in a wide variety of colours to link with a theme.

Taxus baccata hedges (far left), 3m (10ft) in height and 1m (3ft) in depth and width, were planted at intervals on alternate sides of this pathway to lead the eye along its length. As well as framing each section, the way they make the eye bounce from side to side gives the impression that the space is longer than it is.

This pathway (left), leading up to the main garden from the conservatory kitchen on a lower level, was given a strong look with Noce travertine set between cream travertine, creating a decisive vista to the planter and mirror beyond. At night it is highlighted by LED strip lights routed into the underside of each step, producing a lovely lighting effect.

Blockwork-rendered slab walls of different heights (left), painted to tone with the cream paving setts, were placed at junctions along a winding pathway to help divide the space, as well as acting like sculptures that you chance upon as you discover the garden.

I wanted to add some greenery to this tiny courtyard (below) and we did so by planting two frangipani (*Plumeria alba*) in overscaled pots that increase the feeling of space and tone well with the surrounding materials. The trees are taller than the boundary wall, which helps to forge a link with the neighbour's trees beyond, and they cast great shadows onto the pool of water. The flowers have an exquisite fragrance that filters through the entire house via the slatted doors, which allow a lovely view even when closed, as well as ensuring that air can circulate freely.

To create the feeling of more space in the seating and dining area of this garden (right), we used a series of mirrors set into bronze frames that were matched to the existing windows and doors of the house to follow the same architectural detail. This means that even those people who are seated facing the wall while at the dining table will still have a great view of the garden.

For this roof garden (opposite top), I framed a series of three mirrors in timber deck boards, the same as we used for the flooring, because they gave generous borders to the mirrors and also ensured the space had a simple, co-ordinated identity. The mirrors were set on spacers, so that they were slightly proud of the battened trellis fence, with LED strip lights inserted on the reverse all the way around, which gave a great light at night (see page 147). **The timber-clad wall on this roof terrace (opposite below)** was a perfect place to add a timber-edged mirror, as the wall needed something of interest on it. It ensures that anyone sitting on the exterior sofa still has a great view of the overscaled pots placed along the boundary behind them, here planted with a mass of tulips.

The boundary wall of this urban front garden (above) was old and had been repaired many times, so we clad the whole expanse in louvred timber and made a cupboard in the same style, on the right of the photo, for storing the dustbin (trash can), hose reel connected to the outside tap (faucet), irrigation system and hand tools. The mirror placed behind the daybed, which incorporates storage for the cushions, makes not only the bed, but the entire space feel larger than it is, and ensures that everybody has a good view when seated at the table.

CASE STUDY
OPTICAL ILLUSION

We designed this long, narrow garden, leading off the main dining room at interior designer Nina Campbell's home, a number of years ago. We wanted to give an interesting perspective to the space, so we designed the flooring treatment to create an optical illusion that would make the small courtyard garden feel larger than it really is.

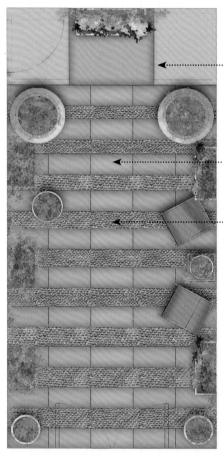

The area to the left is another entrance; the area on the right is for storage.

Buff sawn sandstone alternates well with the black pebbles.

The pebbles were set on their edges into wet cement and then grouted in place. The bands get narrower as you look down the garden, tricking the eye with a false perspective.

The flooring is made up of strips of buff, sawn sandstone, 30cm (12in) wide, alternating with black pebbles, set on edge, starting at 30cm (12in) wide but with each band getting progressively narrower. At the end of the garden is a raised platform, with mirrored panels behind grey-painted metal railings on both sides and at the back to give a greater feeling of space.

Both walls – as well as the wall-mounted pipes and extraction ducts on the right-hand wall – were covered with timber louvres, around 3m (10ft) tall. These were used for climbing plants such as the fragrant *Trachelospermum jasminoides* and one of my favourite climbers, *Solanum laxum* 'Album', which flowers for at least six months a year.

The trough is painted in the same colour as the louvred fence, and the porcelain pots are a similar colour, which unifies the elements and makes the space feel calm. Its clean, soft architectural identity is punctuated by the planting and the simple wrought-iron furniture.

I love the louvred lines of the painted fence as a wall application (above left), but I also love how it relates to the stripes on the floor, which is more about texture and colour.

On the 2-D plan (above) you can easily see how the bands of black pebbles on edge get narrower as they reach the back of the garden, creating an optical illusion that makes the garden look bigger.

This small, narrow garden (opposite) is a delightful place to sit and relax. The space is reflected in the mirrors at the end of the garden and this helps to enhance its sense of volume.

TEXTURES & SURFACES

ROUGH & SMOOTH

It is always interesting in any design to combine complementary materials – in a brotherly/sisterly way. This means you need to think about how the textures will work together, as well as the colours, in order to create a good balance of rough and smooth.

During the early stages of any design it's important to think about how you can bring in different textures. This can be done in so many ways – through boundaries, flooring, containers or features that can be highlighted by lighting at night. Garden lighting tends to draw attention to textural detail, sometimes more than daylight. I tend to use floor washes as a safety feature to highlight steps and changes of levels, and I like the way the low-level lights pick up the surfaces of paths and terraces.

A colour or theme may be the starting point of a design that sets the tone or evokes a feeling within the space, but when choosing materials, make sure you consider texture in relation to how the space is going to be used. Ask yourself whether shoes will always be worn or if the area will be walked on with bare feet, and think about whether the space gets exposed to different temperatures and weather conditions. If so, a surface's slip-resistance may well be an important factor to consider. On one roof terrace we designed (see pages 36 and 176), we used lovely, nonslip, grey porcelain tiles and layered them with a rug in the same colourway, like grey artificial grass, and it is superb to walk on in bare feet. The sofas are upholstered in a soft grey canvas, and the same coloured velvet has been used on the Louis XVI-style chairs, so all the elements complement one another.

The gravel used as a mulch (previous spread) is the same stone as I used for paving the paths, which mellowed with the natural stone walls of the house.

The Cotswold stone wall (above) contrasts well with the relatively smooth texture of the cream clay pots on the Portland stone floor.

Local Mediterranean stone was used to build terraces for these planting beds (left). The same crushed stone was incorporated in the render used on the blockwork wall behind to obtain a similar colour and a slightly textured surface. Both sit comfortably against the hillside.

Different forms of the same type and colour of stone were used to build the water wall for this pool (opposite), together with a narrower, machine-cut stone with a natural-faced front edge for the main wall. The brown tones are picked up by the timber decking and the mosaic tiles lining the pool.

CASE STUDY
TEXTURAL BALANCE

This garden's defining feature is the textural mix used within it. The starting point was the pair of huge plane trees (*Platanus* x *hispanica*) that we had to work around, their trunks about 125cm (50in) in diameter with a lovely, gnarled, bobbly surface, like a burr walnut veneer. The design idea was to divide the space into a series of three 'rooms' that flowed into each other: the lower basement area as a place for exercising outdoors, as it leads off the gym, the middle section for dining and the rear raised seating deck for relaxing.

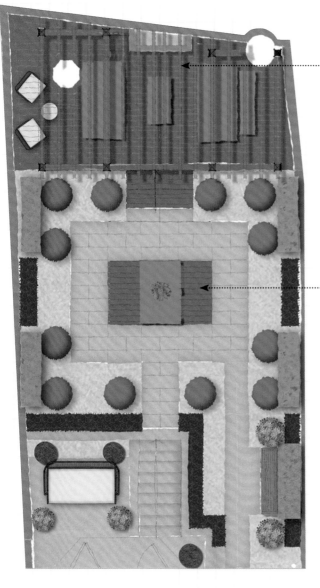

We had wanted to cover the raised decked terrace with a slatted pergola, but we had to omit it due to planning restrictions. We introduced planting beds in front of each tree to soften the space. The texture of the tree trunks provides a lovely backdrop for the plants.

I wanted the dining table to look as if it were sitting on a rug, as you might do indoors. The inset panel of timber decking links well with the raised area and breaks up the large expanse of paving. It is positioned symmetrically between the two pleached trees, together with a panel of yew (*Taxus baccata*) hedging and a further panel of white tulips.

Both of the existing brick walls between the neighbouring properties were only 125cm (4ft) tall, so we ran lovely, smooth, battened Marathi timber fixed onto posts above them. We then added a further layer of screening for total privacy by planting two pleached trees in front of the walls on both sides. This added a leafy texture high up, to help soften the boundaries and give the garden year-round structure.

To tie in with the battened trellis, we placed a raised timber decked area at the back of the garden that would weather to a silver-grey. It created a flat surface over the large tree roots and, being slightly elevated, gives a lovely view over the garden. Buff, sawn sandstone, which mellows well, was used for the majority of the paving, step treads and coping on the low, rendered white walls and the top of the fireplace. In the middle section of the garden, we set a rectangle of timber decking within the stone paving, to look like a rug, onto which we placed the dining table. Defining this area within the space makes the garden feel larger than it is.

Bark mulch was used in the flowerbeds under the rear trees, which looks great with the split-hazel fencing that we alternated with panels of woven willow around the raised seating area. The lower flowerbeds were mulched with Cotswold chippings, to tie in with the sandstone paving. This not only looks good but also helps to suppress any weeds and retain moisture during the warmer months.

Railings had to be added along the stairs and edge of the middle level for safety, but in time the *Taxus baccata* hedge will grow through and disguise them. Many of the plants were chosen for their leaf texture as well as their silver-grey colours that tone with fabrics in the conservatory. One of my favourites, *Hebe pinguifolia* 'Pagei', has lovely blue-grey, spear-shaped leaves and delicate white blooms that fit the colour scheme. It is one of the evergreens that provide year-round interest.

The timber sofa frames will eventually tone down to match the grey webbing. The textured cream cushion covers tie in with the white dining chairs, with their PVC mesh seats. The result is a restful space, which blossoms when all the herbaceous plants fill the spaces after a fragrant start to the spring, with masses of white hyacinths and majestic white tulips.

I wanted a good proportion of evergreens within this symmetrical layout, and a favourite is white *Camellia japonica* (far left) for good winter interest. I love the striking contrast between its glossy green leaves and the spiky grey-green fronds of the yew hedging; the lush, matt leaves of the tulips (centre left and near left) give such a great sense of promise within a garden; and I love the almost black-and-white effect of the white *Tulipa* 'Clearwater' with the leaves of *Sambucus nigra* 'Gerda'.

Cotswold chippings were chosen as a mulch (below left) to provide a good contrasting texture for the buff sandstone paving, as well as being an almost identical colour match. The *Buxus sempervirens* spheres provide further evergreen highlights.

The planting palette (opposite) was kept to a simple green and white with a small amount of aqua-grey in the trees planted on either side of the fireplace, which matches one of the interior fabrics. I love the textural overload of this garden, with the split hazel hurdle edged in a machine-cut timber frame that makes the tree trunk look like a stand-alone sculpture, together with the smooth timber decking boards in iroko and the Roda teak sofa. The textured cream cushions complement the purity of the tulips.

COLOUR & TEXTURE

Texture is almost as important a factor as colour within a garden design. I often choose a combination of different surface materials – and sometimes planting, too – within the same tonal range. This has the effect of making each colour work harder, and shows off the different textures and sculptural qualities of the materials.

A favourite idea is to place rough, natural Cotswold stone against machine-cut Cotswold stone, and put these with either cream limestone or travertine, filled or unfilled, to add a further texture. Set against cream rendered walls, the subtle differences look great together. The same idea can be implemented in a different colourway by using rough pieces of slate with Belgian blue limestone flooring, a zinc water feature and galvanized pots. This makes a great combination with battened trellis painted a duck-egg blue. More often than not, I will choose a muted, tonal base as the mainstay of a theme and then add a punch of colour – or a combination of a few bright colours, with orange and lime-green being firm favourites. If you include reds with this mix,

This entrance to a property in France (opposite), with its lovely water feature, is a good example of tonal colours and lively textures at play. The blocks of Belgian blue limestone used for the walling have been machine-cut on two sides so they can be stacked on top of each other, with the natural rough side exposed on the front edge. The coping of the pool is the same stone but with a smooth, flamed finish. These have been used alongside the grey granite setts of the driveway and a concrete rendered wall with lovely blue-grey *Agave americana* planted along the top edge, to act as a natural balustrade. The colour palette for this lush garden (left) was green and white, and we used all different shades, leaf shapes and sizes to form a really interesting mix of planting, where some plants, such as the *Alocasia*, became architectural specimens planted among a mass of *Syngonium* as ground cover.

PRACTICAL CONSIDERATIONS

• When using mulch on flowerbeds next to grass, try to provide a neat edge, such as metal, so that the mulch doesn't end up on the grass.

• If you have stone pathways going onto grass, make sure you leave a wide enough entry point so that the grass doesn't wear away in one place.

• If you are building a child-friendly garden, bull-nosing the edges of stone steps will give a softer finish.

• When using a glass balustrade, consider putting a frosted logo on it, especially if you have children, as the glass is not always easy to see on a sunny day.

• Avoid having metal steps in hot climates, as you will not be able to walk on them with bare feet.

• Think carefully when using mirrors in an urban environment, especially if there is a high population of birds. Also, be considerate about reflecting sunlight into other people's property.

• When placing screens on roof terraces, be aware of occasional high winds. Battened screens allow the air to pass through easily.

• Always check the load-bearing capacity of roof structures. Timber decking helps to spread the weight over an entire roof. Plastic containers with lightweight compost are ideal for planting.

• Timber deck boards are comfortable to walk on in bare feet, making them a good choice for any areas where you may be barefoot.

• Concrete shuttering is an inexpensive surface that is great for driveways, as it gives a good grip.

they are perceived as hot colours, and you may become weary looking at them for any length of time. Red makes a space seem smaller, so I tend to use hot colours to add foreground colour, and greens, blues and purples to add background depth. Cool greens and blues will often make an enclosed space, such as a light well, feel larger than it really is, but sometimes a darker background colour in a basement can give stronger emphasis to the planting and in turn make the space feel bigger. When using darker colours for paving, such as granite setts, Belgian blue limestone or slate, I tend to use more shades of green for the planting, as this absorbs the colour more easily. Lighter surfaces, such as limestone, travertine and Portland stone, are more reflective and give a much lighter, brighter appearance. All surfaces take on a different identity when wet and will usually appear darker, so stronger foliage colours are better in this instance. I am also influenced by the location of the garden, as the quality of light is completely different in various parts of the world and affects the colour and texture of plants accordingly.

The main design focus of this zen-like garden (above), where there is minimal planting, is the use of colour and texture. I used all the natural colours found within the bark of these pine trees to create the subtle colour changes within the waves of gravel and, because we kept to this very natural palette, the end result is very strong. Nature is so often the richest source of ideas and I believe we should always look at our immediate surroundings to see what inspiration there is to be gained from them.

I laid an apron of Cotswold stone on-edge at the front of this property (left) to stop the gravel being taken into the house and to make more of a feature of the entrance doorway. The apron also gave us a surface on which to position these two reconstituted stone pots in a similar colour, planted with topiary bay (*Laurus nobilis*) and seasonal underplanting, which I wanted to help pick out the colours of the stone mullion window frames and the stone of the house itself, as well as the colours of the log pile in the porch – it's all in the detail.

Green and orange are two of my favourite colours, and what better way to combine them in a contemporary garden (below) than to have orange tarmac paths with sculptured mounds of grass, together with rust-brown and hot-pink floating walls, which create very clean lines and frame up the planting beds. All the natural colours form a soft palette – the green, brown and beige gravel – and adding the punchy man-made orange gives a great contrast and vibrancy to the space.

BOUNDARIES & SCREENS

The choice of boundary material – or combination of materials – helps to define the style of a small garden, so it is always a good starting point for any design. There are so many really effective options to choose from, which all set a different tone and evoke a different mood within an outdoor space, from split-hazel hurdles, woven willow panels or battened trellis – either natural or painted – to plain green hedges, pleached trees or louvred panels with inset mirrors.

I wanted to paint this archway (above) an earthy chocolate colour to help define the space, as well as framing up the planting beyond, like a painting. It emphasizes the change in flooring surface and makes the grass stand out with greater effect.

Pleached *Sorbus* (above) were alternated along the boundary of this garden with flame-shaped hornbeams (*Carpinus betulus*), their changing leaf colour and shape creating an interesting effect. It was important to make sure that all the trunks, which were uplit at night, were in line.

If its design is successful, a garden should take you on a journey without you going anywhere. When you assess your site at the beginning of the process (see page 10), you may find that you need to screen things surrounding your garden, to hide an unattractive view or to help provide privacy from neighbours, for example. Being out of sight from others makes a place feel more welcoming and creates an instant sense of calm. Sometimes attention can be diverted from an eyesore, such as an ugly structure or boundary in the line of sight, simply by some strategic planting of a shrub or tree. Alternatively, screening may be used to create a sense of separation or enclosure. The screen could be a trellis clad with climbers or even a transparent material such as glass.

Boundary screens can take the form of solid barriers – wooden fences, trellis screens or battened panels, for instance. In many countries there is a standard maximum height – usually 1.8m (6ft) – for such screens, which doesn't deal with the problem at hand. Interestingly enough, natural boundaries are more acceptable and there aren't many laws that say you can't plant trees or shrubs to a higher level. In these cases we often use pleached trees, which are basically hedges on stilts and give a very clean line to a boundary.

Trellis offers a convenient way to add texture and colour. In this garden (right) we used it to cover up an existing wall and help screen a neighbouring property from view. The mirror framed within it reflects lovely views of the garden.

The dining table (opposite above) is placed centrally on a decked 'rug' between two pleached trees with a panel of *Taxus baccata* hedging and another of white tulips in front. The linear battened trellis helps make the space feel larger, yet clean and architectural, with a soft, organic contrast provided by the planting.

A series of mirrors placed along this walkway (opposite below) makes the boundary more interesting by reflecting the garden and conservatory. The louvred screens were painted to match the porcelain floor tiles inside and were set in a timber surround to tie in with the mirror frames.

In some cases, planting a series of flat-pruned *Platanus* x *hispanica* trees creates a flat screen overhead, which effectively blocks the view of neighbours looking down onto the garden (see page 88). When used over a seating area, the living canopy gives a magical feeling to the space, and the play of dappled sunlight and shadows cast onto the garden is quite lovely (see page 128).

If it is unwelcome background noise you are wishing to screen, consider adding a water feature (see page 108). The sound of gently moving water can be particularly soothing, while a more effervescent effect will add invigorating energy to the space.

I often like to add features such as arches to gardens, either in the form of timber frames or rendered and painted blockwork. Positioned over paths, they frame the view, creating an effect similar to that of a traditional pergola. It's not always realized that a pergola has a dual effect upon perspective, working both horizontally and vertically, creating two separate areas and the potential for two very different moods. As you walk through a pergola, each of the spaces to either side frames a different view, forming a series of ever-changing pictures along the path. I have found that the apparent space may be extended by duplicating features along the sides of a pergola,

We often incorporate a built-in planter to help soften a wall. This wall (below), which might otherwise be too tall as it descends to a basement level, is further softened by trailing plants over it from the grass edge. It looks impressive when they are in flower and connects well with the planting below. We needed a barrier (opposite top) to stop anyone falling from the ground-floor level of this garden into the basement. To link it in with the overscaled cream pots, I had a metal, cream, powder-coated trough made with clay panels fixed to the front. This was planted with a white camellia hedge along the back with a series of *Buxus sempervirens* spheres and tabletop box.

Planning restrictions for this roof terrace (below) stipulated that people must not be seen on the roof from street level, so we had to erect a barrier that would keep people 1.5m (5ft) away from the edge. We decided to place a series of overscaled, white, rigid plastic pots on the other side of a clear glass balustrade, which was the regulation 110cm (43in) tall and allowed an uninterrupted view. We were able to plant the pots with trees, which helped to give the roof terrace privacy from the buildings on the other side of the street. The fact that we had many pots all along the L-shaped glass barrier gave us very strong boundary planting, so the rest of the planting could be on a smaller scale.

such as repeat planting. This effect is further enhanced by placing a sculpture or specimen plant at the far end of the main axis, creating a focal point, which may be lit up at night for extra drama. Floating walls of different heights, placed at angles, and evergreen plants trimmed into architectural shapes are other vertical planes I like to add to gardens to provide good winter structure.

This wonderful pergola of green oak (above) has arches running along the side as well as over the pathway and is covered with cascades of climbing roses and other heavenly scented climbers, with alternate panels of *Lavandula angustifolia* 'Hidcote' and *Nepeta* 'Six Hills Giant'. The water tank below the lead lion's head was built from reclaimed bricks. **The beech (***Fagus sylvatica***) arch (right)** frames the view to the flame-shaped hornbeams, which were planted along this old-brick boundary wall as a high-level hedge. In spring its branches have a sculptural quality and in the summer its purple leaves contrast well.

CASE STUDY
TREILLAGE GARDEN

The original idea for this particular garden was to incorporate vertical structures, as we wanted it to be a fusion of French style but in a modern form, using interesting materials. The aim was to design a garden that would look architecturally pleasing but at the same time be a space that the whole family could use and enjoy.

Trellis has been used in many famous French gardens to help create rooms, walkways and vistas, and here we used it to emphasize the grid shape that we also used for the upper paving. This forms a central square of tumbled cream travertine that is also a water feature, with nine colour-changing jets of water. Having the stone tumbled gave it a French feel and made it look slightly antique. The trellis columns are placed in pairs with a linking arch, and there is a series of three arches along the back wall, with the centre one being mirrored. Defining the space with sections of trellis already makes the garden feel bigger than it is, and the addition of the mirror takes this one step further.

The glass balustrade that runs along the front edge of the garden's upper level ensures safety while allowing a completely uninterrupted view of the entire space. We were also able to fix an LED strip along its base where the glass is clamped into its housing, which creates a great lighting effect along the edge of the glass. When looking out from inside the house, this edge-lighting looks more and more amazing the higher up you go.

The mirror at the end of the central vista (right) leads the eye into the garden, with the majestic trellis columns framing the view. The four quarter segments around the water feature are for seasonal planting, together with four sections of artificial grass. **We divided the rectangular garden (opposite)** into three spaces – dining, lounging and an activity area on the upper level. The glass balustrade almost disappears, giving an uninterrupted view of the whole garden, yet ensuring safety at the same time.

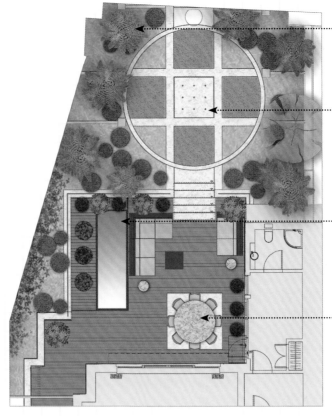

We planted tree ferns to represent palm trees on the Côte d'Azur.

The child-friendly water feature has nine colour-changing jets of water within squares of cream travertine paving.

The rectangular glass panel slides under the timber decking to reveal a staircase to the basement pool.

The table stands on a square of cream travertine set within the timber deck to look like a stone 'rug'.

The lower level of the garden is divided into two sections – a seating area and a dining space. A square of tumbled travertine set within the timber decking marks the position of the bespoke French-style circular table. As the kitchen opens onto this space, we chose the same stone for the garden tabletop as had been used in the kitchen for the worktops, creating an echo between the inside and outside spaces. To further emphasize the French theme, we chose a set of French lattice-style dining chairs with lime-green exterior cushions. To increase the sense of space in this area, we used pieces of mirror, the same size as the glass doorway and with the same bronze detail as the windows, and repeated them along the wall so they appeared to be part of the architecture of the building, rather than an addition. This is effective, as you are never sure where the house ends and the garden begins.

In terms of the planting, the tree ferns were a play on the palm trees that you see on the French Riviera. I love the old, gnarled stems of the olive trees, planted in the large-rimmed clay pots and underplanted with lavender and *Muehlenbeckia complexa*, with its great stem and leaf structure. The shrubs in this garden are white-flowering *Camellia* as well as *Magnolia grandiflora* and a great selection of honey-coloured *Heuchera*

'Marmalade', *Helleborus* and orange *Fritillaria*. Spheres of *Buxus sempervirens* in varying sizes migrate through the garden in both the beds and pots, adding to the year-round, evergreen effect. This is added to by the four panels of artificial grass, alternating with the four sections of seasonal planting, seen here in spring comprising two different types of tulips, *Hyacinthus orientalis* 'Gipsy Queen', red primulas and red and burgundy violas.

The lower section of the garden (left) is used for relaxing on sofas and for dining. We lined up the central vista from the table right through to the mirrored arch on the centre of the back wall on the upper level. The locked glass gate makes sure the staircase to the basement pool is kept safe at all times. **The summer seasonal bedding (top left)** consists of *Nicotiana*, burgundy trailing pelargoniums and red *Impatiens*, mulched with Cotswold chippings. A great backdrop is provided by the trellis column and the tree fern and box spheres. The seasonal planting is changed twice a year and the entire colour scheme is changed once a year. **Spring seasonal bedding (top right)**, which follows on from winter violas, consists of apricot *Hyacinthus orientalis* 'Gipsy Queen' and a mix of red and orange/yellow tulips. The wonderful reflection in the mirror has the effect of doubling the quantity of flowering blooms and lush foliage. **In some of the other containers (above left)** we planted *Helleborus* with *Hyacinthus orientalis* 'Gipsy Queen', burgundy violas and apricot-coloured primulas. **I adore the leaf shape and colour** of this *Heuchera* 'Iced Tea' (above right) against the clean sphere of *Buxus sempervirens* and the early summer orange flowers of a *Fritillaria imperialis* behind it.

UNDERFOOT

Flooring surfaces are among the most important features in the design of a modern garden. Whether they are paving, lawn, gravel or timber decking, they must always possess the qualities of particularity and precision – that is, the materials must not only be right for the site, but they must also be used in the right way.

Using just one type of flooring material throughout a garden – and perhaps even continuing the same or similar flooring from the adjacent interior – can help to unify the space, whereas introducing a different type of flooring will instantly change the mood and can be used to indicate a shift in activity or zone. I particularly like the striking contrast of cream travertine stepping stones through vibrant green grass, as it creates a sense of energy and invites you to walk through the space. I often like to designate an area within a terrace as a dining space. An inlay of timber decking within stonework, for example, changes the pace and provides a place for the table to stand; the decking takes on the appearance of a 'rug' and helps the garden feel a lot more spacious. This device also works in reverse, with a stone 'rug' placed within timber decking to set off a dining table and give the area a sense of place within the overall landscape. The same idea can also be achieved simply by changing the direction of the timber boards within a larger decked area. This is a great way to break up a large expanse of decking and make it look more interesting.

When choosing a flooring surface for a garden, it is very important to consider whether it is likely to be walked on barefoot, especially when the garden is located in a very hot climate. If this is the case, avoid dark grey or black materials, such as slate, granite setts or black granite, which tend to soak up the heat and are sometimes impossible to walk on. Lighter-coloured materials seem to hold less heat, so go for cooler limestone or travertine. Timber decking feels wonderful underfoot, but only the smooth deck boards, not the horrible ribbed ones.

Squares of stone set within grass (above left) can be used to create a softer-looking path. This is a useful solution where you occasionally need access for a vehicle, for a delivery for example, and a lawn would not be sustainable. **Artificial grass (above right)** was used to help break up a harsh environment of painted walls and railings, to give a softer look to what was an exposed and open roof space. Rows of pots planted with various cacti add further interest.

I like to place wide panels of grass in between narrow decking boards (above left), as I love the colour contrast. Here, both materials sit very comfortably alongside random-sized pieces of natural stone. **Creating curved decked paths (above right)** is not easy, and here we have planted along its edges to divert the eye and disguise the decking detail somewhat.

I liked the look of these brick-edged pebble inserts (above left), but when I walked across them to the front door of the barn, I found that they weren't a very pleasing surface underfoot. So, to create more of an 'Arts & Crafts' feel (above right), we laid York stone in various squares and rectangles with cream-coloured handmade bricks in basketweave designs of different sizes at the edge, together with lots of random planting pockets within the paved areas and groupings of old, weathered terracotta pots, giving the whole area a rustic feel.

In warm countries it is often necessary to leave expansion gaps between paved areas to allow for movement, and in some cases where you also get heavy rainfall at times, you may well need a series of drains. In this garden (right) the opportunity was taken to create a nice design detail by adding pebbles to divide up the paving. It looks great from above, as the width of the pebble details are similar to the width of the various walls – any narrower and the result wouldn't have been as effective.

To change the pace in the dining area, the timber decking of the seating areas gives way to rectangular pieces of a lovely flamed-finished Belgian blue stone in a running brick formation, which looks very clean and modern. We designed the white Carrara marble dining table to tie in with the white stucco architecture of the house, and this choice of material brings an immediate feeling of luxury to the space. We then placed a line of five large clay pots, planted with *Buxus* spheres to look very architectural, against the glass balustrade surrounding the basement garden, creating a lovely place to have lunch on a sunny day.

The main, L-shaped garden looks down onto a lower garden at basement level, where we placed a taller version of the water feature used in the main garden, together with another pair of large, rimmed, clay pots, planted with 4–5m- (13–16ft-) tall *Cornus kousa* var. *chinensis*. These beautiful, tall specimens help to link the two spaces together.

I love to have successional seasonal planting in pots, as we did in this garden with white hyacinths, followed by white tulips for spring (previous spread), and then lilies and lavender for summer. The rest of the garden is a mixture of strong evergreens and architecturally shaped trees. The mood board (above right) is all about the different textures and surfaces we wanted to use within this garden, from the hard materials, including grey stone, timber decking and the white Carrara marble side tables and dining table, to the upholstered chairs, together with *Buxus* and *Echeveria* planted in Cotswold chippings, which were also used as a mulch. The raised water feature (below left) is set against a mirror,

flanked by two overscaled, cream, double-rimmed clay containers planted with *Cornus* and seasonal underplanting. The line of cream clay pots planted with *Buxus* spheres (below right) work well on the terrace, as well as looking interesting from the French windows opposite, as the glass balustrade allows them to be seen clearly. I like the way they line up with the dining table and its series of central table decorations. We changed the pace for the dining area (opposite) by paving it in grey stone. This is enhanced by the charcoal-grey rug on which the white Carrara marble table and white moulded-plastic chairs sit. The surrounding mirrors reflect the garden, so everybody has a great view wherever they are sitting.

FEATURES & FOCAL POINTS

POOLS, PONDS & WATER FEATURES

I like incorporating water into any size of garden, as it introduces movement, sound, light and reflection, which all contribute to the overall sensory experience. As a natural element, water works well in any environment and can often disguise surrounding noise; it will also help to energize and refresh the atmosphere, and will add a magical quality to any garden or space.

It's not easy to find great-looking hot tubs, so this one (above) was installed on a roof as a built-in design. We planted the *Elaeagnus* x *ebbingei* hedge for privacy, but it also has wires running through it to stop anyone from falling off the roof, creating a green balustrade. This pool (right) was lined with lovely square mosaic tiles of pale grey-blue stone, to match the stone walling, which makes the water reflect the colour of the sky. We chose the fabric for the sunbed cushions and parasols to co-ordinate with the stone, as well as the *Eucalyptus gunnii* and *Cedrus atlantica* Glauca Group that were planted along the left of the pool for screening.
The gentle sound of water pouring from the line of central jets into this long, ornamental pool (previous spread), combined with the heat and scent of the pine trees on the level above, is quite magical.

This clean-lined water feature (right) was inspired by La Grande Arche de La Défense near Paris and we have used it in many gardens over the years. The pipework required to convey the water from the trough at the bottom to the metal hopper at the top is built into the blockwork wall, which has a piece of glass (frosted, as here, or coloured) attached to it. Running water over glass creates minimum splash, so it is ideal for a small space. The timber edge doubles up as somewhere to sit and play your hands through the water.

A long, shallow pool of water (below) was created opposite the front door of this property to distract the eye from the supporting wall that was so close to it and which now serves as a textured backdrop to the pool. With its simple jets of water, it creates a calm, welcoming atmosphere – and there are great reflections on a sunny day.

When designing a garden in a warm climate, the main consideration for your space could well be a swimming pool, plunge pool or hot tub. If the garden is not very large, this may result in you having only a small area left for planting, which means that it will have to work extra hard to create an effect.

Introducing a pool or water feature into a garden instantly creates an atmosphere and defines its mood. I love the play of light and dappled reflections upon water, and looking down onto it is cooling and relaxing. The sound of gently moving water is satisfying and reassuring, and can be particularly soothing if it helps to block out other, less welcome background noises. On the other hand, a large, gushing water feature can have the opposite effect on the mood of a garden by generating a sense of drama and excitement.

There is a water feature to suit any style of garden, whether traditional or modern. Sometimes I like to juxtapose the two, perhaps giving an old-fashioned circular pool a modern centrepiece, such as a zinc sphere with water cascading over it, or incorporating a reclaimed stone or lead spout into a contemporary design. A water feature may be used to provide a focal point to draw the eye and ear, or act as a tranquil backdrop. A rill of water running through a garden encourages a pause for thought and can also play a strong role in creating perspective. This device dates back to early Islamic gardens, where low, rectangular pools of water and fountains were linked by narrow canals.

On this modern roof terrace (top left), we mounted an old lead hopper reclaimed from Manchester Fire Station on the old brick wall and added a lead pipe from which water cascaded into a rectangular pool made of glass bricks (chosen to tie in with glass-brick walls inside the property). Loose pebbles placed in the bottom disguise the pipes and pump. Lit up at night, it looks and sounds magnificent, and I love the juxtaposition of the modern and the old. Jets of water on either side of the stepping stones (top right) add a cool layer to this internal courtyard and create lovely shadows of rippling water on the walls. A traditional, vase-shaped stone fountain (above left) gently bubbles water from a central spout into the circular pool below, which we edged with lavender for a simple, rustic look. This square, metal, powder-coated water feature (above right), with its central jet, also acts as an interesting planter, with a *Buxus sempervirens* hedge all the way around it.

The central rill of water (left), leading up to a circular pool at the end, reflects the sunshine in between these two large panels of lavender. I love the contrast between the textured finish of the steps and pathway against the rough stone walls on either side and the slightly smoother paving used for the terrace.

CASE STUDY
POOLSIDE LOUNGE

It was a joy for us to help create interesting outdoor spaces for this delightful farmhouse in France. We approached the design with a less-is-more philosophy and took our lead from the materials that had been used for its construction, choosing complementary materials that would work well with them.

To work with the existing interior levels, we needed to create a raised terrace along the long barn wall. This required us to build a low wall, which gave us one side of the pool. This was a perfect place for a change of level, so we had steps built into this wall, as well as two reclaimed spouts, which allowed us to circulate the filtered water back into the pool.

Terracotta tiles had been used inside the house, so we also chose them for the terrace, with two rectangles left out to plant a pair of old olive trees that gave the space a sense of time and place. These and the cypress were underplanted with purple *Iris germanica*, to give a sense of formality and to help define the seating area. Pairs of overscaled square zinc planters further define the space. Zinc patinates beautifully and works well with the house's painted shutters, creating a very cool, calm palette of colours, especially when planted with prostrate rosemary and lavender.

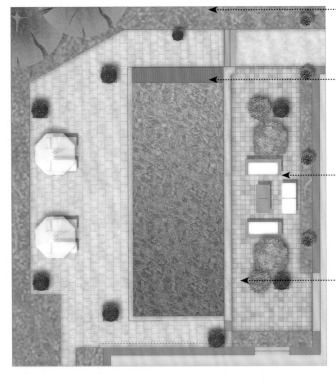

The border is a mix of shrubs, some evergreen, to give a year-round effect.

The timber cladding stores the automatic pool cover used to retain heat and keep it clean in the winter.

The furniture was chosen to link in with the colour of the stone of the house, but also to give a contemporary feel.

Reclaimed terracotta tiles define the seating area, differentiating it from the stone-paved area around the pool.

The large, boxy furniture and pairs of overscaled zinc cubes (right), together with the olive tree, work well with the very upright habit of the *Cupressus sempervirens* Stricta Group. The golden evening light casts wonderful shadows and reflections onto the pool (opposite above). The simple water jets in the raised wall are reminiscent of a typical French sink. The patinated zinc cubes (opposite below) are a good colour match to the house's painted doors and shutters. Together with the textured stone walls and warm terracotta tiles, they create a soft palette, complemented by the silver-grey olive trees and lavender. I love the vertical lines of the *Cupressus* (overleaf), which have an air of authority over the gnarled olive tree, but I also love the prostrate rosemary cascading over the zinc cube.

ORNAMENTS & FOCAL POINTS

Even in the smallest of outdoor spaces I often try to create a view or vista, and I will frequently position a focal point at the end of it to draw the eye. This could be a simple evergreen, such as a topiary *Taxus baccata* or a *Laurus nobilis*, or if the budget permits, a sculpture, either freestanding or placed on a rendered blockwork or zinc plinth. I particularly love the organic shapes of Tom Stogdon's ammonite sculptures made from Cotswold stone. Alternatively, an interesting pot planted with seasonal colour might work well, positioned either as a focal point or within the space as a central feature. A statue, tree, topiary or other evergreen, with seasonal planting, set within a *Buxus*-edged square planter and surrounded by pathways, makes a great central feature for a small front garden.

This Shaun Brosnan sculptured head in beaten lead (left) is displayed prominently on a zinc plinth, and I adore the way the white-flowering *Wisteria* surrounding it looks like its new hairdo.

I love to use natural stone as a garden sculpture, and within this garden (top) a 1.5m- (5ft-) diameter Cotswold stone circle by Tom Stogdon has been set on a 3m- (10ft-) wide *Buxus* plinth, which is uplit at night, and creates a wonderful view at the end of a vista of stepping stones.

In the middle of this rill (above) we had a very shallow pool of water where we were able to position this great, sculptural figure, which is uplit at night. I love the clean lines of the pleached trees as its backdrop, underplanted with rows of *Buxus* balls.

This ammonite-shaped sculpture, carved from Cotswold stone by Tom Stogdon, is placed on a white rendered plinth in the planting bed at the end of the garden, directly opposite the doors to the ground floor interior. When you walk into the garden, it acts as a visual focal point, leading you up the steps to discover what is beyond. The natural material in a very organic shape works well in a contemporary garden.

Occasionally we are asked to incorporate key pieces or sculptures that the client would like to use within a garden design. One such piece was an amazing giant golden apple (see above), which we placed in front of a window that looks out over the garden from the downstairs toilet. Positioned between two tall clay pots, planted with *Buxus* spheres to complement its shape, the apple acts as a focal point along the length of the wall and brings a real zing to the identity of the garden.

One item that I often like to include within our small garden projects is an exterior fireplace. As well as being a welcome practical addition to a seating or dining area, a fireplace can also be used as a focal point. Sometimes I will make it the central focus for a seating area, at other times I might position it as an end point to a vista. A fireplace provides a great opportunity to create a space divider, which can be used to define zones within a rectangular garden. A floating wall, rendered and painted white or a colour that continues a theme in the rest of the garden, can be used to house a double-sided fireplace, with an outdoor room, each with its own style or mood, on either side.

Background planting can also be used to create a focal point. Sculptural topiary, a tall or ancient tree with an interesting shape or texture, or a splash of bold colour will all draw the eye.

The golden apple sculpture (above left) reminds me of Adam and Eve in the Garden of Eden. The gold finish ties in well with the cream and Noce travertine paving, the latter having a golden hue. The opening of this double-sided fireplace (top right), built into the white rendered freestanding wall towards the end of the garden, lines up with the trunk of the tree on the far side, which gives shade to a seating area. The cobbled path in front defines the panel of grass. The area behind the wall changes pace, from formal to relaxed, with a looser style of planting. There is also a garden shed in this working end of the garden among the soft planting. The hexagon within this paving design (above right), which lines up with the entrance to the property, was crying out for a central feature, and the Allison Armour sphere fountain, Aqualens, with water cascading all over it from the centre top point, was the perfect scale to link in with the rows of planted box spheres. Keeping to just *Buxus* and the bamboo (*Phyllostachys nigra*) created a very strong contemporary identity alongside the white rendered walls and grey window frames. In this enclosed courtyard (opposite), we punched an oval-shaped hole through the perimeter wall and exposed the bamboo planting beyond, thus giving the space a great focal feature. The addition of the 'borrowed' greenery within the space helped link it with the water hyacinths growing in the low bowl in the foreground.

GARDEN ROOMS

SHADE & SHELTER

I think all garden structures play an important role, whether they are purely decorative, such as a pergola or arch to frame a view or define a zone, or functional, such as a shed for storing garden implements, furniture and barbecues, or somewhere to shelter from the heat of the sun or the rain. Either way, they need to fit in with the overall design of the garden.

Gazebos, summerhouses, pavilions and even humble sheds are undeniably useful structures to have in a garden, whether they are used for dining, relaxing, working, spending time on a hobby, or arranging flowers and potting plants. These buildings come in a range of styles, from traditional to contemporary, or they can be designed from scratch to suit your requirements. Whether ornamental or purely practical, a building can form an integral part of a garden's design if it is positioned as a focal point within the space – to help emphasize a vista, for example.

Storage space is always an important consideration in any garden, however small, as it is essential to have somewhere dry to keep all the tools needed to maintain the garden. Try to incorporate this within an aspect of the design, such as under built-in seating or raised timber decks.

Trellis has been used for many years – to add height to boundaries, to create screens or simply to provide climbing plants with a foothold. I truly believe it's going to make an even bigger comeback in the years to come, as it's a cost-effective way to add a decorative structure in any size of garden.

My favourite covered space is this lovely L-shaped built-in bench with grey velvet cushions on the roof of this house (previous spread). It's a great place to recline and read, or for a host of people to chat and enjoy the view. The built-in planter is edged with a hedge of *Elaeagnus* x *ebbingei*, with the foreground planted with white-flowering agapanthus and a front line of prostrate rosemary, which has white freesias flowering through it in the spring – absolute heaven. **The charming 'Langton Pavilion' (left)** has timber shales on the roof and walls made from overlapping panels with a double door and a beautiful circular window.

We designed the 'Gail Pavilion' (left) as a slatted, open-roofed structure with a false wall, which is partially clad in smoked mirror, behind which is a storage shed.

The 'Jasmine Porch' (below) is a simple but elegant timber-framed structure in green oak that we designed and added to this lovely old barn, together with the green oak pergola. I adore the way the plants are growing so well out of the planting pockets within the paving of the courtyard, giving the whole garden a rustic identity.

Lovely linear shadows are cast by the slatted walls and roof of this pool loggia (right), and we linked this in with the slatted sofas we chose for the location, as well as the spiky *Astelia* plants that seem to work well to help create the overall identity of the space (see also pages 134–7).

This oversized daybed (below) works very well as a focal point at the end of this grey resin-bound pathway. The central square coffee table with its grey stone top is surrounded by hydro-draining cushions in one of our 300 exterior fabrics and sheltered by a Perspex roof that we added to the structure to extend the season in which it can be used. White muslin curtains can also be drawn around the four sides to give privacy as well as shade at different times of the day. I like the way the tall, linear pots stand guard on either side. They are planted with *Westringia fruticosa*, which we keep clipped into spheres, to give a great link to the surrounding planting. I love the upright habit of the *Cupressus sempervirens* Stricta Group behind the structure.

The 'Nils Pavilion' (left) has a partially slatted roof structure and a back wall constructed from timber offcuts, which looks like a piece of art, together with its exterior lampshade. The steps going up to this pavilion are also clad in timber to keep a co-ordinated feel to the garden, and they work well alongside the white rendered walls.

This open barn (below) makes a superb drawing and dining room with the lovely exposed timbers, natural stone walls and simple terracotta tiles. It will provide shelter in the winter and keep you cool on a hot summer's day. The glass-topped table and cream-coloured fabrics keep the style of the whole space very light and simple – the only thing I would like to add is a chandelier over the table.

This slatted timber pavilion (below) works really well as a yoga space. It gives lovely dappled shade on the deck, as well as allowing the breeze to flow through it, and it also provides a layer of privacy and containment without losing the lovely countryside setting among the frangipani and almond trees.

If space allows, sometimes it's fun to create a sheltered courtyard within a garden by building a wall and putting a false front door into it. Anyone arriving at the doorway, especially if it's at the front of the property, assumes it's the front door to the house, but it actually leads you into an enclosed garden with a further doorway beyond. This could be used as a kitchen garden or to grow delicate plants that require a sheltered environment in order to thrive. We created a magical entry like this at a house in Ibiza, where a double wooden door in a Mediterranean garden leads you down some stairs to a charming, semi-enclosed garden.

In a warm climate, you may wish to create a partially enclosed space for sheltered outdoor dining, perhaps with a fireplace – which could be gas or gel in an urban environment – to enable you to eat outside much later in the season. This could be a freestanding structure or one that is built onto the side of the house or an outbuilding.

If we are involved in a project sufficiently early in the design process, we often like to create a shady spot that forms part of the architecture of the house. At one Mediterranean property, we worked closely with the architect to form a concrete canopy that extended out from adjacent rooms. Timber decking was laid beneath the

Here I wanted to create natural shade when the *Platanus* x *hispanica* are in leaf (below). The idea is to train them along the cane structure so that they meet, together with a third planted in the raised square planter, to create an L-shaped canopy. It was also desirable to give a layer of privacy to the garden, as there is an apartment block that looks down onto it, and the flat-pruned nature of these trees helps to block out the view from above.

I particularly like the architecture of this house (above), which has both a rustic and modern feel. The concrete overhangs above each decked area are a great design, as they form perfect shadows in the heat of the day, as well as providing shelter if it happens to rain. The mix of materials is very successful against the natural stone walls.

canopy to give the rooms their own outdoor zone, each of which was furnished with a pair of cream clay pots, planted with barrel cactuses, and a table and chairs or sunbeds, creating a series of mini outside rooms. In another garden we designed in France, the clients opened up one side of an old barn to use as a dining and lounge space, which offered protection from the heat of the sun as well as from rain or wind.

Sometimes it's more appropriate to the brief we've been given to create structures within the garden spaces themselves to provide shade. These may be in the form of a pergola, a freestanding umbrella or a structure with upright stone or brick posts, over which a fabric canopy can be added for the summer season.

I always try to create some natural shade in a garden, too, particularly over a dining area, as it's usually more comfortable not to be in full sun when you're eating outside. Palm trees are a lovely way to provide natural shade in a hot climate, with a table and chairs placed beneath to take advantage of the dappled sunlight and magical shadows that move gently in the wind. Palms bring an architectural identity to a space and can be underplanted with herbs or other plants that need a shady spot to do well. Sometimes we use flat-pruned trees, such as plane trees (*Platanus* x *hispanica*) for warm climates, which respond well to this treatment. In an urban environment they not only provide welcome shade, but also give privacy from neighbouring buildings.

When designing this smart poolside terrace (above), we went to a lot of trouble to make sure we used the same colour canvas for the blinds (shades) and for the seating cushions. In addition, the housing for the blind was colour-matched to the paint chosen for the exterior walls of the house.

INSIDE OUT

Whenever you're working with a small garden, it's a good idea to treat the entire space as an outside room. This allows you to create a garden that you are able to enjoy as much as possible as an extension of your interior, both to look at and to spend time in relaxing, cooking or cultivating plants – whether you want a dedicated area to grow your own vegetables or herbs, or just a few attractive containers of architectural plants and seasonal colour within the space.

This roof terrace (above) has an awning made from a simple metal frame with fixed slatted timber panels, which give great shadows. It covers only half of the space, so it is possible to sunbathe if you wish. We chose the slatted sofas to tie in with the theme, which is further echoed by the slatted timber decked floor.

The dining area in this rectangular garden (above) is defined by decking, while the rest of the garden is paved. The wooden louvres of the boundary can be open or closed, depending on how much light and/or privacy is required. The glazed pots of acers tie in with the cushions on the plastic Bubble Club sofa and armchair by Kartell.

If there is room to create several areas within the space you have, you may decide to have an outside kitchen with a dining space as well as an area to relax in, or you may wish to turn most of the garden over to planting, depending on your priorities and the effect you wish to achieve.

Protection from the sun is always an important consideration when creating outdoor rooms and I love using different methods to achieve this (see page 122). A metal framework can be a great way to define an outdoor seating area, particularly in an exposed space such as a roof terrace. Shade from the heat of the sun can then be provided either by attaching a canvas cover that can be removed at the end of the summer or by using timber battens as a roof. This is a favourite method of mine, as it produces lovely shadows while making the space beneath feel like an enclosed room. On the other hand, in milder climates, being able to remove the canopy allows you to make the most of any winter sunshine. Try to make sure that such a structure isn't positioned over the planting, so that the shade it produces doesn't affect the growth of the plants. To furnish the space beneath, we usually use freestanding furniture or long, built-in benches, topped with hydro-draining cushions that can be left out all year.

We designed this garden (above) especially so that we could use the great wraparound, U-shaped sofa. There is a built-in raised flowerbed along the back of it, together with a staircase to the left and planting on both sides, so the space feels like an enclosed drawing room with a natural canopy of flat-pruned *Platanus x hispanica*. The hydro-draining cushions can be left outside all year and can be sat on a few minutes after rain. We have more than 300 exterior fabrics, from velvets to chenilles and linens in both plain and printed designs, so we can choose one to link with almost any interior fabrics.

Don't forget that something as simple as planting a tree may give you all the natural shade you require, especially in a small courtyard garden. We will often make the most of an established tree by positioning a dining table and chairs beneath it. As well as giving protection from the sun, its branches can be decorated with nightlights in the evening, as well as crystal drops that glisten alluringly in the sunshine and create a lovely twinkling effect as they move in the breeze.

Always try to assess your space with an open mind, as you may well find that you have a redundant area or feature that can be turned into something useful. On one roof garden that we designed, we were able to transform some existing old chimney stacks into two fully functioning exterior kitchen spaces. The fronts were broken out and double doors were inserted, then the interior of one was fitted out for cooking – with grills for fish, meat and vegetables, including a teppanyaki griddle – and the other with an outside refrigerator, together with a sink and storage for plates and glasses (see also page 144).

This roof-terrace kitchen (above) sits really well in front of the planter of *Elaeagnus* x *ebbingei*. The plant's silvery green tone looks great with the grey worktops, while the wooden doors tie in with the timber slatted roof that provides essential shade and good ventilation when using the barbecue. The olive tree in this delightful courtyard (opposite) was originally planted in a flowerbed. The area was covered with dark grey polished concrete and a table was added around the trunk of the tree, creating a magical place to dine in candlelight, with the light reflected off the crystal drops hanging from the branches. The terracotta pots work well with the soft colour of the exterior walls.

One city garden we created (above left and right) had an open space at the front of the property, which had to serve as the main garden and create a sense of arrival, so we decided to design it as a multifunctional area. A tiled path leads from the gate to the front door, and the same tiles continue into the hallway of the house to help blur the boundaries between inside and out. On one side of the path, two built-in planters hold a pair of semi-mature magnolia trees. The area between the planters was clad in timber to form a daybed (above right), with storage underneath for cushions and gardening tools. The black pots link with the black dining furniture on the other side of the path. Between the planter and the house is a cupboard to store dustbins (garbage cans), and this also houses the tap (faucet) for the semi-automatic watering system. The boundary wall was of poor quality, so we clad some of it in timber battening and inserted a large mirror to give the space a feeling of greater depth. On the other side of the path we laid a raised deck, so that you could walk out of the house on the same level as the interior. This is where we placed the black glass dining table and Panton chairs, with a side-supporting black canvas umbrella (above left). A series of *Olea europaea* helps break up the line of the boundary, while a hedge of *Elaeagnus* x *ebbingei* turns the black railings into a green screen.

OUTDOOR LIVING

Sometimes in a garden where the location is known for having a longer season and the weather is fine for most of the time, we find ourselves designing several outdoor rooms in different areas. An exterior living space might lead off the interior one or a place for dining off the kitchen. There may also be other areas for entertaining or lounging, such as beside the pool, if there is one, or even in the smallest of places, such as on a roof terrace. This dramatically extends the usable living space and means the clients can really make the most of their garden.

I love this raised dining area (above), which is 'framed' by a row of three pots placed on plinths on either side. Atop the crisscross Perspex base, the grey stone tabletop matches the paving stones, giving a very clean, simple identity to the whole space.

In this lovely property in France, we created several outdoor rooms for the owners to enjoy. A small roof space off the bedroom was decked over and then we built a simple slatted timber canopy on a steel framework, which creates shade and lovely shadows; it also helped to raise the balustrade up to the legal height above the parapet wall in a very neat and tidy design. The pair of sofas, with a series of coffee tables made from stone cubes between them, makes a lovely place to relax and admire the view.

We followed this same methodology at the end of the swimming pool, but this time we used the slatted timber panels for the back wall as well as the roof, with bamboo planted behind it, which gives a lovely shimmering effect as the light shines through. Behind an

The pool's filtration allows the water to cascade down a water wall, helping us to deal with the changes in level.

The water from the outdoor shower drains through the timber decking.

The grey/white resin-bound gravel pathway adds another texture to the garden.

The machine-cut stone blocks look like art but function as coffee tables.

This garden (left) is a whole series of rooms, leading from one to another. Here, you can see that by going down the steps to the lawn, this will lead you to a further set of steps that take you down to the pool level. We have used *Elaeagnus* x *ebbingei* as balustrades at the top of the walls, which helps to give privacy to the pool area.

The pair of sofas facing each other over the stone blocks makes a great relaxed seating area (above). The dining area beyond is defined by a pergola frame, over which *Wisteria sinensis* 'Alba' is growing, to give a natural shady canopy; it will be magical to dine at this table when the wisteria is in flower – and it will smell heavenly, too.

L-shaped sofa we created a simple outdoor shower, with the drainage built under the timber decking so the water drained away in the same way as a shower on a boat. We had used stone blocks in other areas within the garden, so we also introduced them around the pool as occasional tables to continue the theme.

If I were to choose my favourite covered space in any garden I have worked on, it would be the large terrace on the roof of this property, which is edged with planters and a generous-sized, L-shaped, built-in bench (see page 120). We introduced another series of eight stone blocks, which looks like a contemporary art installation but doubles up as a functional coffee table. There are also Louis XVI-style occasional chairs that can be pulled up to the blocks to make a low table for informal dining.

We repeated this idea of the series of eight stone blocks on the main terrace within the garden, which extends along the back of the house and overlooks the garden and pool, but here they sit in between a pair of large sofas facing each other. Beyond this lounge area is a lovely, long, wooden slatted dining table under a canopy, which can be used for formal entertaining. Still further along the terrace is a third area for more casual dining for smaller groups of up to four people. The circular tabletop, which sits on a Perspex base, is made from the same stone as we used for the flooring of the terraces. Three cream pots, planted with domes of flowering lavenders and placed on plinths, create a lovely vista.

The woven cocoon on this roof terrace (above), which leads off the bedroom, is a great place to escape to and read a book. We placed the row of three pots planted with *Agave attenuata* in front of the boundary to link with the greenery in the distance, and I love how simple and yet architectural they are.

This slatted pool pavilion (below) was designed not only to give shade, but also to provide privacy from the neighbours, as well as acting as a fence to stop you falling down the hillside. The sunbeds can easily be pulled out into full sun should you wish, or you can sit comfortably on the L-shaped sofa in the shade. Here I used the same stone blocks as side tables to tie in with the rest of the garden.

FURNITURE & FURNISHINGS

I think the furniture and furnishings are a very important part of designing any garden because whatever size of space you have, the furniture either needs to be in the right scale or overscaled, if the space allows. It's necessary to be practical about how you want to use the garden, so think about whether it's a space for entertaining and, if so, how many people you need to seat for dinner, or whether it's to be used for several different functions – relaxing, chatting, having meals in, cooking and sunbathing, for instance.

FAVOURITE FURNITURE

A string chair on a metal frame, such as this Harp chair from Roda, makes a simple but effective design statement. I often add a base cushion.

I love the simplicity of the Root table from Roda, with its grey high-pressure laminate (HPL) top and primitive-looking wooden base. I often use it as a side table.

The Pier table from Roda is a smart powder-coated metal table base (in a choice of colours) with a slatted timber top. It's the perfect lightweight dining table.

A simple slatted timber coffee table is both useful and practical.

A Louis XVI-style armchair and footstool upholstered in exterior-grade fabric bring interior comfort outside.

Any garden furniture needs to be durable, as in most locations it will be exposed to varying types of weather, from being cold and wet to hot and sunny. Be aware that often things are labelled as being waterproof when in reality they are only showerproof, so it's worth investing in quality products that are what they say, otherwise you could spend a lot of money on something that will only look good for its first season. We do a lot of research into this aspect, as we don't like to disappoint clients.

Moulded plastic has advanced considerably in recent times, and over the years the quality has improved a lot. It is an ideal choice for a family garden where children are likely to be charging around and the furniture needs to be very durable and hard-wearing, able to withstand bumps from bicycles, as

The lounge seating in this multipurpose outdoor space (below left) is all one style – high-quality plastic Bubble Club by Kartell. It works well with the slatted timber dining table and chairs, and the clean-lined glass balustrade, which keeps everything light and airy. **We choose this great, white, powder-coated metal table** with a wooden slatted top (below right) to tie in with the white mesh dining chairs with wooden arms, as they co-ordinated well with the cream canvas cushions on the sofa.

This lovely curved oak sofa called Splash, from Gaze Burvill (bottom left), is a beautifully handcrafted piece, which gives a contemporary feel to a garden as well as a sense of craftsmanship.

These sunloungers with hydro-draining cushions (bottom right), are perfect beside a pool, as the slatted shelf is ideal for towels.

I do like built-in benches (above), which enable us to build planters into the wall behind. Together with the panels of cream canvas strung between the posts to create shade, these add to the sense of enclosure. The cushion fabric was also used for the cushions on other seating within the garden. This small city garden (below) easily accommodates a colour-themed dining area for six to eight people. The specially dyed orange canvas umbrella provides shade over the pink slatted table and purple chairs, which tie in with the alliums in the concrete rings.

well as children climbing all over it. Moulded plastic furniture can be made to look very smart by adding your own customized cushions, which could easily be changed each season to make the garden feel new and different.

Sometimes the style of garden may cry out for furniture that has a sculptural quality. On an African-themed roof garden we designed (see pages 34–5), the two chairs at either end of the dining table were solid blocks of oak with brushed stainless-steel backs, chosen to represent the thrones of an African tribe's king and queen. They worked well with the simple benches we made from lengths of rustic timber fixed onto metal legs. The 'throne' chairs also complement the zinc-wrapped dining table; zinc is a metal that oxidizes well, which meant it also co-ordinated with the torn strips of lead used for the sculpture we designed in various shapes of African tribesmen's shields, which were set within the black reflective pool of water.

I often like to co-ordinate the colour, material or style of the furniture with the overall feel or design of the space, as we did in a city garden furnished with a pink-painted slatted wooden table surrounded by purple chairs and shaded with an orange umbrella (opposite below). These were the three accent colours that we used elsewhere in the garden – in the planting and as neon rings of light around the bases of the oversized containers. The full complement of colours looked great against the grey backdrop, and the cut flowers inside the house were of the same colours to further emphasize the theme (see also page 44).

Another favourite design that can be adapted to suit different themes is our 'floating' tabletop placed on a crisscross Perspex base (below left), which ensures the table doesn't look too heavy within a small space or interrupt the view of the garden. The tabletop can be of various materials to suit your theme, such as stone to match the terrace on which it sits, or marble to echo and link with kitchen worktops inside the house.

Always consider all the materials and tones within the garden to ensure your furniture fits in. For instance, in one garden (below right), a slightly weathered concrete bench was chosen to sit on the Portland stone terrace, as its colour co-ordinated so well with the flooring. It also looked great against the overscaled cream clay pots, which had a richly textured finish. It can often take time to find the right pieces that complement each other, but when you do it's very exciting to see how the furnishings can bring the whole space together.

Sometimes the smallest of spaces can be transformed into lovely, generous-sized seating areas, especially if you can incorporate a change of level into the space, perhaps with steps down into the seating area, which could be surrounded on three sides by lush, fragrant plantings. One of my favourite seating options are L- or U-shaped sofas, which often work well to form a large seating area at one end of a roof terrace or courtyard. Together with an awning or some form of natural canopy overhead, and perhaps with a slatted or louvred timber screen behind or built-in planters forming a boundary, they can be used to create a semi-enclosed outdoor living room. It's a good idea to co-ordinate the colours of the cushions to work with the interior fabrics, perhaps including some accent colours to bring out the colour of surrounding planters. A soft, neutral palette in shades of cream and taupe on wa pale grey base cushion, which works well with zinc cube planters, always looks chic.

The crisscross Perspex base of this small dining table (above left) makes the tabletop – here black marble – appear to float so the table doesn't overpower the space. The Louis XVI-style dining chairs, upholstered in a chic stripe, can be left out in all weathers. **I have used this style of bench in timber many times,** but this example (above right) is cast-concrete, hand-finished and coloured, and looks beautiful with the oversized textured clay pot behind it. **When a garden is divided up with a series of flowerbeds** edged with *Buxus sempervirens* (overleaf), it can feel like a series of different rooms within one space. Placing a dining table in one area creates a cosy, secluded place to eat.

CASE STUDY
ROOFTOP LOUNGE

This is one of my favourite roof gardens. The space has a few limitations within which we had to work, but we ended up with four quite distinct spaces, which all worked well together, maximized the available space and made it a great outdoor area for all the family to use. I love the way the glass roof over the top of the stairs slides across itself to give access directly onto the roof, which also means there is a lot of natural light flooding down to the space below. The only drawback is that you can go onto the roof only when the weather is good, otherwise you could have water cascading down the stairs. Behind this is space for a barbecue to be installed.

The entire roof was covered in a lovely hardwood timber decking, but I wanted to define the central seating area, which I designed as if it were a drawing room, so we used a charcoal-grey exterior rug. On this we placed a pair of taupe cord sofas with matching taupe cushions, facing each other over a pair of stone-topped coffee tables. (Now there is also a large umbrella, which covers the whole of this central space.) At the narrow planter side of this seating arrangement is a freestanding heater and at the opposite end, a pair of Louis XVI-style armchairs, to tie in with the French theme seen throughout the house. Behind this is a self-contained white glass-reinforced plastic (GRP) water feature, which has a clear Perspex cover to go over the top, so that it can be used as a side table on which to set down drinks or a tray if serving tea on the terrace.

At either end are additional seating areas in front of former chimney stacks, which we converted into two outdoor kitchens. In one we installed a small bottle refrigerator, worktops and a sink. A small dining table and four chairs make a cosy, sheltered place to enjoy lunch or dinner. At the other end of the terrace is a pair of sunloungers opposite the second part of the exterior kitchen, which houses the hob and grill with built-in extraction. Both the kitchens have painted battened doors, to match the battened-trellis panels that provide wind protection and privacy. We echoed this idea, but in natural wood, for the fronts of all the perimeter planters. To meet safety regulations, we had to add an additional barrier at a height of 110cm (43in) to stop people from climbing onto the containers and getting too close to the edge. To prevent this barrier from looking too intrusive, we chose metal pots with steel cabling, which allowed the plants to grow through it, so the final effect is quite soft and it almost disappears.

We defined the main seating area (opposite) with this great, dark grey exterior rug onto which we placed the lounge furniture. There are two coffee tables so that it is possible to place a large rectangular umbrella between them, which covers the entire seating area.

The entrance is through a sliding glass cover. Three pots inside and out blur the boundaries.

A flush skylight set into the decking allows natural light to flood down into the hallway below.

A Perspex-covered, self-contained water feature in front of a central mirror.

One of the two outside kitchens with painted battened double doors.

I chose this pair of sunloungers (top left) because the slatted bases match the slatted planters behind, and the grey webbing on them also ties in with the theme as an accent colour. I always like to add cushions in the same fabrics that I have used on other pieces of furniture, as I have on this sofa (top right). It strengthens the theme you are creating as well as making the furniture more comfortable. The painted battened double doors to one of the pair of kitchens in the old converted chimney stacks (above), with their decorative shell handles, give a nice backdrop to the milk-coloured frames and taupe cords of the chairs. I particularly love the palette of materials we put together for this mood board (left). The taupe, grey and white colourway makes a neutral and soothing backdrop; the shell door handles add an opulent feel; and the granite used in the two exterior kitchens matches the kitchen worktop in the house.

Lit up at night, the chimney stack kitchens (right) glow like sculptures. Here, we see the cooking unit with its extraction hood, and the antique mirror splashbacks (backsplashes) that were chosen to tie in with the French theme.
LED strip lights behind the frames of the three mirrors (below) give a great effect, as do the uplights directed onto the clear-stemmed and cloud-pruned *Olea europaea*. With the addition of small directional spotlights illuminating the coffee tables, the combination of lighting on this rooftop creates a lovely ambience for relaxing and enjoying the sunsets.

PLANTING

THE GLORY OF PLANTS

Plants can often give a garden everything it needs in the way of structure, style, personality and year-round interest. Sometimes trees play a vital role in the architecture and design of a garden – by this I mean they can often form boundaries and enclose a space. I always love to use what I call a hierarchy of plants, so the trees and hedges are considered first, followed by the shrubs and climbers, then the herbaceous perennials and, lastly, the bulbs and annuals – the seasonal plants such as spring bulbs or summer bedding.

Whatever size of garden you are designing, it is very important that you produce a planting specification for it. To enable you to do this successfully, you will need to have already established the orientation of the garden, whether it is exposed, which areas, if any, are sunny or shady, and what type of soil it has – ideally, knowing what its pH level is.

Once all these aspects have been determined, you can select the right plants accordingly. People often make the mistake of having too many different varieties of plants, and this is where my less-is-more philosophy applies. Of course, you want to try to achieve year-round interest, especially in a small garden where you have a smaller space to work within. In this case, you will need to choose plants that tick more than one box and have several characteristics, such as flowering in the spring or summer and having good winter colour or interest. It is also important to think about plant characteristics if you wish to

Great, gnarled *Olea europaea* (**previous spread**) seem to march through the parallel lines of plants with their green and silver foliage. Lines of red-flowering *Freesia* along both sides of the path add colour and fragrance. **I planted** *Cornus kousa* var. *chinensis* **between two pathways** (**opposite**) as a focal point and to balance two slab walls nearby (see page 69). As a foil for its loose style, I added sculptural *Buxus sempervirens* spheres with mounds of *Hebe pinguifolia* 'Sutherlandii', and planted *Allium hollandicum* at random. **Wide flowerbeds complement this wide gravel pathway (above),** leading the eye to the urn. I love this mix of green and silver foliage awaiting the summer blooms.

add fragrance, choose evergreens, create shade or good ground cover, or attract wildlife into your garden. In recent years I have noticed that more people, mostly those with families, are wanting to grow their own produce. Incorporating vegetables, herbs and fruit in the garden is a great way to get youngsters to understand where food comes from and how it is grown – and nothing tastes as good as home-grown produce. Some varieties of vegetables don't mind being what I call 'companion planting', but certainly vegetables such as carrots, potatoes and cabbages need a dedicated space within a garden.

On either side of the arches on this house's façade (below), we planted lovely mature specimens of *Cupressus sempervirens* Stricta Group to give definition to the space. In between we placed a series of three cream clay pots planted with *Agave americana*, which have such a strong architectural look.

MY TOP 10... *(in no particular order)*

TREES
- *Betula utilis* var. *jacquemontii*
- *Betula nigra* [1]
- *Carpinus betulus*
- *Ceiba speciosa* (formerly *Chorisia*) [2]
- *Cupressus sempervirens* Stricta Group
- *Eucalyptus gunnii*
- *Nyssa sylvatica*
- *Olea europaea*
- *Platanus* x *hispanica*
- *Quercus ilex*

HEDGES
- *Bougainvillea*
- *Buxus sempervirens*
- *Elaeagnus* x *ebbingei*
- *Fagus sylvatica*
- *Griselinia littoralis* [3]
- *Ilex aquifolium*
- *Ligustrum ovaliflolium*
- *Nerium oleander* [4]
- *Taxus baccata*
- *Teucrium fruticans*

SHRUBS
- *Camellia* (white cvs) [5]
- *Eriobotrya japonica*
- *Hydrangea paniculata*
- *Magnolia* x *soulangeana*
- *Osmanthus fragrans*
- *Phyllostachys nigra*
- *Pittosporum tobira*
- *Syringa vulgaris* [6]
- *Viburnum opulus* 'Roseum' [7]
- *Viburnum tinus*

SEASONAL PLANTS/ FLOWERS
- *Calendula*
- *Dahlia* [8]
- *Freesia*
- *Galanthus nivalis* [9]
- *Hyacinthus*
- *Impatiens*
- *Lilium*
- *Narcissus*
- *Tulipa*
- *Viola*

HERBACEOUS PERENNIAL
- *Agapanthus* (white cvs) [10]
- *Alchemilla mollis* [11]
- *Anemone* x *hybrida* 'Honorine Jobert'
- *Euphorbia characias* subsp. *wulfenii*
- *Geum* 'Borisii'
- *Helleborus niger*
- *Hosta sieboldiana* var. *elegans*
- *Iris*, Bearded cvs
- *Paeonia lactiflora* 'Shirley Temple'
- *Stipa gigantea*

ARCHITECTURAL PLANTS
- *Agave americana* [12]
- *Agave attenuata* [13]
- *Brahea armata*
- *Cupressus sempervirens* Stricta Group
- *Cycas revoluta*
- *Dicksonia antarctica* [14]
- *Ilex crenata* – cloud or niwaki pruned
- *Pinus pinea*
- *Plumeria* (frangipani)
- *Tetrapanax papyrifer*

SCENTED PLANTS/ FLOWERS
- *Brugmansia*
- *Chimonanthus praecox*
- *Clerodendron trichotomum*
- *Convallaria majalis*
- *Gardenia jasminoides* [15]
- *Hamamelis mollis* and *H.* x *intermedia*
- *Philadelphus* x *purpureomaculatus*
- *Salvia officinalis* 'Purpurascens'
- *Thymus* [16]
- *Trachelospermum jasminoides*

TREES
Betula nigra [1]

TREES
Ceiba speciosa [2]

HEDGES
Griselinia littoralis [3]

HEDGES
Nerium oleander [4]

SHRUBS
Camellia (white cvs) [5]

SHRUBS
Syringa vulgaris [6]

SHRUBS
Viburnum opulus 'Roseum' [7]

SEASONAL PLANTS/FLOWERS
Dahlia [8]

SEASONAL PLANTS/FLOWERS
Galanthus nivalis [9]

HERBACEOUS PERENNIAL
Agapanthus (white cvs) [10]

HERBACEOUS PERENNIAL
Alchemilla mollis [11]

ARCHITECTURAL PLANTS
Agave americana [12]

ARCHITECTURAL PLANTS
Agave attenuata [13]

ARCHITECTURAL PLANTS
Dicksonia antarctica [14]

SCENTED PLANTS/FLOWERS
Gardenia jasminoides [15]

SCENTED PLANTS/FLOWERS
Thymus [16]

SEASONAL PLANTING

We often incorporate seasonal planting within our designs, as it's a great way to bring different colour schemes into the garden throughout the year. Each year I love to involve our clients in the selection of spring bulbs at various garden shows, where we are able to come up with a new theme or colourway to work with.

In the autumn, we are busy planting up containers with spring bulbs. I always try to mix hyacinths with tulips, which tend to flower in that order, and if we add crocuses, they are the first to bloom. I often plant winter pansies (*Viola*) around the edge of containers, so the pots don't look too bare during the winter months. Always mulch the pots with gravel in a co-ordinating colour – not only does this make the pots look more attractive, but it also deters squirrels and mice from digging up the bulbs, keeps moisture within the pots and helps prevent weeds from growing.

Summer bedding, which is the key seasonal planting in any size or style of garden, can range from hanging baskets, to the planting of *Geranium*, *Impatiens* and *Nicotiana*, to the sowing of annuals, which, together with summer-flowering lilies, give a riot of colour right through to the first autumn frosts. Dahlias are one of my favourite summer flowers, as they produce a great succession of blooms for a long period of time – the more you cut them for display inside the house, the more flowers appear. I also often pot up whatever is in season at the time to place in the centre of a dining table.

Old French laundry buckets (top right and below) make perfect containers for seasonal planting in our French-themed garden. The patinated grey metal looks great with both the spring-time blue and pink hyacinths and the autumn planting, which consists of the central, tall *Anemone* x *hybrida* 'Honorine Jobert', together with *Sedum telephium* 'Purple Emperor' and *Gaultheria mucronata*, with its amazing pink berries. The planting in this front garden (above left and right) is welcoming at any time of the year. Here, in the spring, we have rows of bulbs, such as *Tulipa* 'Fontainebleau', *Tulipa* 'Dordogne' and *Hyacinthus orientalis* 'Gipsy Queen', which pick up the colours in the resin-bound pathway and the red brick of the house. Once the bulbs are finished, you are able to see the rows of plants more easily – *Heuchera* 'Marmalade', *Uncinia rubra* and assorted evergreen ferns in rows. This style of planting is inspired by Dutch bulb fields.

These four images are almost a story through the four seasons, starting in spring with *Narcissus* 'Thalia' (top left), which I love against the stems of *Betula utilis* var. *jacquemontii* and the leaves of *Digitalis pupurea* f. *albiflora*. This is followed by *Polygonatum multiflorum*, which is a favourite of mine, with its arching stems of tubular white bells. **The flower stems of the *Stipa gigantea* (top right)** look very majestic alongside *Iris* 'Deep Black', the lovely glaucous *Allium karataviense* and *Lavandula pedunculata*, which picks up the colour of the iris. **Under the *Betula utilis* var. *jacquemontii* (above left)** we planted groups of *Lavandula pedunculata*, with the great purple foliage of *Salvia officinalis* 'Purpurascens' and *Heuchera villosa* 'Palace Purple'. **In among the leaves of the *Eucalyptus gunnii* (above right)** we have clumps of *Heuchera* 'Marmalade' with the foliage of *Alchemilla mollis* and flower heads of *Euphorbia characias* subsp. *wulfenii*.

CASE STUDY
SEASONAL GARDEN

When we designed a new garden for this house, the first challenge was to screen the driveway and garages from the path leading to the front door, which we achieved by planting a row of pleached hornbeams with a hedge of *Taxus baccata*. We also wanted to create a series of 'rooms' that you walk through as you travel around the property.

I wanted to create a small, enclosed garden to the right of the main stone path. This can be seen from the dining room, as the window lines up with the central square we created for a zinc plinth to display an ammonite-shaped sculpture by Tom Stogdon, made out of pieces of tumbled Cotswold stone.

For many years this side of the garden had been a section of poorly maintained lawn under quite a dense canopy of large trees. Yet the main kitchen-cum-breakfast room looks out onto this narrow strip of land, so we wanted to make it much more interesting. We took the centre of the bay window as the focal point and created a central flowerbed, into which we placed a square self-contained water feature. On either side of this bed we had resin-bound pathways, while up against the hedge we placed tall,

overscaled pots planted with seasonal flowering to give an injection of colour. The area around the water feature itself provided another great place for seasonal planting. The colours of the spring bulbs were picked out from artworks hanging on the kitchen walls.

To the left and right of the central bed are three connecting beds, all edged in Corten steel, into which we planted a series of *Dicksonia antarctica*. The beds are edged with *Buxus sempervirens* and also contain rows of *Buxus* spheres, which link with the rest of the planting in parallel rows. I like putting architectural-shaped evergreens with *Dicksonia antarctica*, which are so majestic and soft in appearance. The beds are mulched with Cotswold chippings, adding another layer of texture and contrasting strikingly with the green of the planting.

I love the architectural **quality** of the *Dicksonia antarctica* (above), with its husky bronze stem, which is almost fur-like.

An ammonite-shaped sculpture made from Cotswold stone by Tom Stogdon (opposite below) is displayed on a zinc plinth, making a focal point in the central flowerbed. Many years ago my parents took me to Keukenhof in Holland, which has the most magnificent spring bulb displays, and it was the Dutch bulb fields that inspired me to start my linear planting style, shown here with different varieties of tulips (*Tulipa* 'Fontainebleau' and *T.* 'Dordogne'), which provide wonderful spring colour.

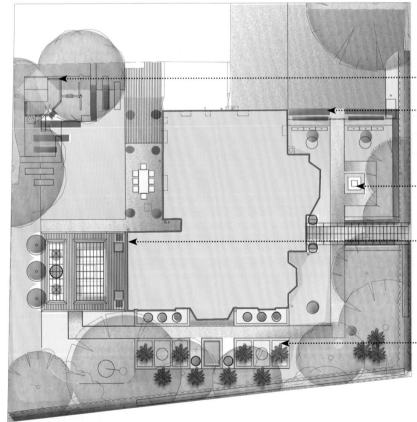

Children's summerhouse surrounded by a rubber play surface.

Screen of pleached *Carpinus betulus*, underplanted with *Taxus baccata*.

Ammonite sculpture on a zinc plinth.

Raised timber deck, with water jets within the paving, and a stone 'rug' with sofas on top.

Rectangular beds of *Dicksonia antarctica* and pink spring bulbs around the zinc water feature.

Iris 'Kent Pride' (top left) is one of my favourite Bearded irises, as I adore its rich colour. *Uncinia rubra* (top second from left) is a great evergreen perennial sedge grass. Cotswold chippings are the perfect choice of mulch to set off its rusty orange colour. *Iris* 'Maid of Orange' (top second from right) sets any garden alight and works particularly well with Corten steel, whether in the form of a sculpture, a driveway edging or a planter. **This** *Euphorbia amygdaloides* 'Purpurea' (top right) works really well with the irises, as it flowers just before them and the old flower heads still give a good foliage base for the other planting.

SCENTED GARDENS

Fragrance is one of the most evocative elements you can introduce into a garden, as it can conjure up a certain time and place, or a special occasion or event. I love to try to use scented plants in as many of our garden designs as possible, since as well as bringing images and memories to mind, it can help to create a soothing atmosphere and encourage moments of contemplation. In many of the Mediterranean gardens we design, there is more often than not a large number of naturalized pine trees around the garden boundaries. In the heat of the summer they give off such a lovely fragrance, which always reminds me of hot summer days, as does the scent that wafts off large groups of lavender, rosemary and santolina.

For the same reason, I like to plant herbs, either within an area that is totally devoted to them or as part of a scheme. There is nothing better than using fresh herbs from the garden for cooking, and brushing past purple sage, walking on thyme plants as they grow over a pathway or touching lemon balm – which doesn't look much as a plant but makes up for that with its intoxicating fragrance – is a treat for the senses. There is a whole range of decorative mints (*Mentha*) and I guess my favourite has to be *Mentha x piperita* f. *citrata* 'Basil', which is highly scented and has reddish tinges to the leaves and mauve flowers. Another good choice is *Mentha suaveolens* 'Variegata' (pineapple mint), which has attractive variegated leaves – and I generally don't like variegated leaves.

Winter is a time when I like to have fragrance to offer an element of surprise in a garden. *Mahonia aquifolium* is a great evergreen with lovely clusters of yellow flowers that smell like lily of the valley. Another favourite is *Sarcococca humilis*, a clump-forming shrub that I often use as a ground-cover plant; it will tolerate pollution and partial shade but has a very sweet fragrance. For a larger shrub, you may choose *Hamamelis mollis*, with its yellow ribbon-like flowers, or *Chimonanthus praecox*, which has unusual flowers and the best fragrance I have ever smelt, like a delicious, slightly spicy French perfume.

To help create a medieval theme for this garden (above), to tie in with the lovely old timber window frames of the property, we planted this narrow flowerbed, 1m (3ft) wide, with *Buxus sempervirens* balls and squares of different herbs, mixing colours as well as leaf forms along its length.

In the spring, there are a selection of bulbs that offer great colour and scent, such as *Hyacinthus* and slightly more subtle *Narcissus*. These are followed in the summer by *Philadelphus*, *Wisteria*, assorted roses, lavenders and herbs. There is also *Clerodendrum trichotomum*, which has exquisite white flowers on layered branches and is often used as a feature tree or within a larger planting scheme.

In the autumn, it always surprises me that when the leaves are falling from the *Cercidiphyllum japonicum*, you get a lovely, rich smell of strawberries crossed with burnt sugar.

Brugmansia suaveolens (below left) has a great architectural identity, with its hanging, scented flowers, and I often use it in Mediterranean gardens. **This is my favourite colourway** of *Nerium oleander* (below second from left). I adore its branching habit and use it whenever the climate allows. **Lily of the valley (below second from right)** has sturdy stems of small bell-like flowers with a fragrance second to none. It naturalizes well, once settled, and is ideal for country-style gardens. *Trachelospermum jasminoides* **(below right)** is a favourite evergreen climber of mine, with lovely clusters of scented white flowers, which can be quite intoxicating.

I deliberately planted these groups of lavender and rosemary close to the flowerbed edges, along both sides of this pathway (above). When they grow over the path during the summer months, you can't help but brush past them as you walk by so that they release their heavenly fragrances.

CASE STUDY
THE SENSORY GARDEN

I created this Gold Medal-winning garden at the RHS Chelsea
Flower Show in 2002 for Merrill Lynch. The Ben Nicholson-
inspired water wall, featuring the sun and moon, is the focal
point at the end of the garden. The meandering grass represents
an umbilical cord – the start of human life as we know it – and
Stephen Cox's wall-mounted sculptures symbolize the five senses.

The main structure of the garden is created by the grid of beautiful, flame-shaped hornbeams (*Carpinus betulus*), which give it a very majestic feel, together with the blockwork rendered wall, with its set-back panels for displaying each of the granite sculptures representing the five human senses. The colour of the wall works well with the two limestone terraces at each end of the garden. The front terrace has a shallow water feature set within the paving, to millimetres of precision, so that it looks like a mirror of water. The water flows over the edges of the stones into a deep tank below, which echoes like a cave. Great drifts and swathes of planting curve up either side of a decent-sized lawn. My favourite elements of the planting are the *Carex buchananii* interplanted with *Allium hollandicum* 'Purple Sensation'.

The sculptures by Stephen Cox were positioned on each recessed section of the rendered wall (below left). I love the way the trunks of the flame-shaped *Carpinus betulus* seem to march in parallel lines through the plot. In the end, I decided against installing the curved timber path dissecting the grass, as it would have interrupted the flow of the garden.

The grey granite of the Stephen Cox sculptures representing the five senses, this one being 'taste' (opposite top), looks wonderful set against the white rendered boundary wall.

First thing in the morning is a wonderful time to be in a garden. I adore how the early morning sunshine lights up the *Verbascum* 'Helen Johnson' (overleaf), as well as silhouetting the simple limestone bench at the edge of the terrace.

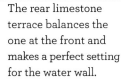

The rear limestone terrace balances the one at the front and makes a perfect setting for the water wall.

The curved path of timber decking meanders through the planting and gives good access for garden maintenance.

A grid of 25 flame-shaped *Carpinus betulus* gives an instant architectural identity to the garden. This was the first time these trees had been exhibited at the Chelsea Flower Show.

The rendered wall was painted in a shade called Vanilla Bean, chosen to match the limestone terraces.

Water is pushed up through a tray holding the limestone paving and poured over the metal edge into a holding tank underneath, which is 1.5m (5ft) deep and echoes like a cave.

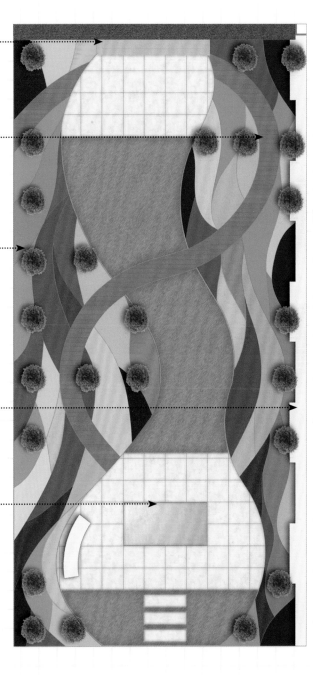

TRADITIONAL & FORMAL PLANTING

This style of planting has been around for many years and, although there was a shift towards more contemporary planting styles at the beginning of the twenty-first century, it is still very popular. The layout of a formal scheme gives a garden structure, while the planting conjures up a romantic and timeless feel.

If space permits, a typical arrangement will see the garden divided into four separate flowerbeds with narrow pathways in between them. A feature is often placed at the intersections of the paths, and seats, sculptures or urns on plinths at their ends. The flowerbeds are usually contained within low hedges of either *Buxus sempervirens* or *Lavandula* and can consist of shrub roses, standard wisterias, clusters of peonies and other herbaceous plants. Keeping a simple symmetry and repetition will help to create a traditional formal style.

Herbaceous borders, first introduced in the Edwardian era, were popular for many years, but they can be expensive and labour-intensive to install and maintain. Most gardens today are not large enough to appreciate their scale.

Shrubs have great ornamental value, as they provide form, colour or texture. They are so adaptable and there are so many species and cultivars available that you will always find a shrub even for the most difficult of situations. One important consideration is their final size, as you need to allow enough space for them to grow naturally. Shrubs such as magnolias, viburnums or camellias can make good focal points within

The irises (above) were added as underplanting to the existing walkway of pleached *Carpinus betulus*. We also added the low wall on the right-hand side, as the ground sloped so much that soil was forever washing out of the flowerbed and down the path. The wall resolved this problem, as well as providing a lovely place to sit and admire the garden. It also forms a strong architectural detail that takes your eye to the top of the path and encourages you to go and discover what's beyond.

This formal rose garden (left) was edged with a low hedge of *Buxus sempervirens*. A pathway with stone columns and a slatted timber roof for the climbing roses to grow over runs along its length and leads up some steps to a raised terrace.

We laid this pathway of old, reclaimed bricks (above), keeping narrow flowerbeds on either side to allow for climbers to be grown up the lovely stone walls and for plants to grow over the edges of the brickwork path to soften it. The low stone wall on the right was built as a double layer, so that soil could be added to the gap in the middle to create a raised planter for banks of lavender and saxifrages. To help break up the large expanse of Cotswold stone, I planted a lovely rambling rose on the gable end of the building. Clear-stemmed, flame-shaped *Carpinus betulus* mark the cross-section of the pathways halfway down.

small gardens. Some shrubs produce lovely flowers; one of my favourites is *Hamamelis* x *intermedia* 'Jelena', the orange-flowering form of witch hazel, which smells amazing and also has great autumn colour. Shrubs also grow well in containers, making them ideal for roof gardens or stand-alone specimens.

I tend to use climbers, especially evergreen varieties, within all styles of planting. Two of my favourites are *Garrya elliptica*, with its crinkly-edged leaves and lovely silver-grey catkins in the winter, and the long-flowering *Trachelospermum jasminoides*, with its glossy, green leaves and white flowers with their heady fragrance. Other favourites are clematis, which come in a wide variety of colours and amazing seed heads; honeysuckles, such as *Lonicera japonica*, which I adore for its fragrance; and *Hydrangea anomala* subsp. *petiolaris*, which thrives in shady spots and produces cascades of white flowers, with a winter structure that is equally appealing. I love to use wisteria for its hanging, fragrant flowers, and in warmer climates I will often grow it for its leaf coverage, to form natural shade over a dining or seating area.

Roses are, to my mind, one of the most traditional plants around. They are popular because they can be used effectively in so many ways, and are available in such a wide range of colours and with many different fragrances. You will always find a variety to suit any colour scheme, whether it's a bush, ground cover or climber. Roses work well in a mixed border, along with shrubs such as *Philadelphus, Deutzia*, lilacs, lavenders, *Santolina*, rosemary and other herbs. I am also using more roses in our Mediterranean gardens, as over the years I have found some varieties that work particularly well there, such as *Rosa* 'Tynwald'.

Bulbs also suit this style of planting. Drifts of snowdrops, which appear from as early as late January in the UK, are a personal favourite, especially with yellow aconites. In spring, wherever possible, I love to see *Narcissus* growing through grass, as well as carpets of bluebells naturalizing under trees, and clumps of tulips and hyacinths in the front of a mixed border. These can be followed in the summer by lilies, alliums, *Eremurus* and then nerines. In early autumn, colchicums and the autumn crocus, together with the miniature *Cyclamen hederifolium*, are great choices for bringing late seasonal colour to the garden.

In this formal courtyard (opposite right) all the beds are edged in *Buxus sempervirens* and filled with a lovely assortment of herbaceous plants – a selection of *Primula, Euphorbia griffithii* 'Fireglow', *Carex buchananii, Salvia officinalis* 'Purpurascens', *Lavandula angustifolia* 'Hidcote', *Agastache foeniculum, Foeniculum vulgare* 'Purpureum' and *Phormium* 'Platt's Black', with a lovely old *Olea europaea* in the central bed.

This formal front garden (above left) is a symphony of cream and green. Cream clay containers planted with spheres of *Buxus sempervirens* are placed on panels of Cotswold chippings and Belgium blue limestone, and set against a backdrop of pleached *Carpinus betulus* underplanted with *Taxus baccata* hedging.

Flanking this conservatory doorway (top) are two great examples of 'lollipop' *Taxus baccata* topiary underplanted with assorted herbaceous plants in oversized clay pots. Two zinc cube planters, chosen to match the colour of the drainpipe, also dress these wide York stone steps with a mix of herbs and lavenders.

This lead-style cube planter (above) gives an Elizabethan feel to the spiral *Buxus sempervirens* topiary placed on the pavers of this formal garden. The beds are also edged with *Buxus sempervirens*.

CASE STUDY
TRADITIONAL GARDEN

I originally trained in classic English garden design, but over the course of my career, as I travelled the world working on various commissions, I have been able to experiment and diversify, changing the planting styles according to the project's location and the native plants available to me. In this tranquil formal garden I was able to revisit the more traditional style of my early work, using elements such as symmetry and repetition, while still approaching the planting in an innovative and exciting way.

The original approach to the property was inconvenient and had no sense of arrival, so we extended the driveway and created a parking area screened from the house by a bed planted with assorted evergreen shrubs. This made a lovely approach to the house, and there are many different routes you can take to the front door. On a hot summer's day you can't fail to notice the lovely fragrance released by the flowering lavender, purple sage, thyme, *Santolina* and *Helichrysum*, all mixing into a heady concoction. The landscape is chalk, so we were able to use locally sourced flint gravel for the pathways, and I love the texture and colour of this against the lovely, old, weathered red-brick walls and York stone paving, and it also set off the panel of grass well.

The main structural planting in this garden is the four parallel hedges at the ends of each of the main beds, together with the L-shaped inner hedges of *Buxus sempervirens*. In the beds in the corner of each 'L', we planted a standard *Elaeagnus* x *ebbingei*, which produces fragrant flowers in January and February. All the other plants were allowed to grow naturally and spill over the pathways, giving them lovely soft edges. Although the overall style of this garden is quite formal, its planting makes it feel very organic and natural.

We were very lucky to be able to use the surrounding trees as our backdrop, so the garden only had to grow a little before it felt authentic and seemed as if it had been here for many years.

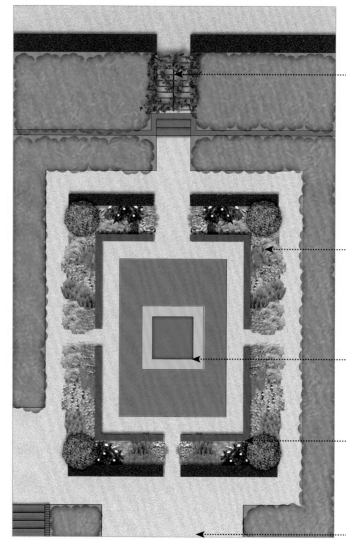

The rose arbour leads you from the parking area to the central pathway.

Each L-shaped bed is a mirror image of the one opposite; its strength is in the mix of leaf forms, flower shapes and colours. A corner topiary *Elaeagnus* x *ebbingei* provides winter structure.

The simple pool has a stone perimeter to link with the gravel paths and ensures grass cuttings won't go into the pool.

The inner side of the beds are edged in *Buxus sempervirens*.

Walking through this formal garden is a great way to approach the front door all year round.

The plants grow over the edges of the beds in a relaxed way (opposite top), forming an irregular border for the gravel paths. The central vista (above) takes your breath away, with the square pool, the formal beds and the loose structure of the planting; the surrounding trees, as borrowed landscape, provide shelter. *Alchemilla mollis* (top left) is a long-term favourite and suits many styles of garden. *Lavandula angustifolia* 'Old English' (top second from left) must be picked when in bud if you want to dry it. *Zantedeschia aethiopica* (top second from right) grows in clumps and has pure-looking flowers and lush, fleshy leaves. *Onopordum* (top right) is one of my favourite architectural plants.

LOW-MAINTENANCE GARDENS

As part of a brief, I am often asked to design a garden that is low-maintenance and, to be honest, it's pretty difficult. All gardens require some maintenance, otherwise Mother Nature will take over and they will soon become overgrown and untidy, as a weed is really only a plant in the wrong place. When you are restoring a garden or designing one from scratch, it's sensible to consider how much time you are able to spend maintaining and looking after it. Do be realistic about this, as even in the smallest garden, the complexity and quantity of planting can prove quite difficult to care for. Once you become accustomed to a particular regime of maintenance, you can always increase the plant varieties – and therefore the work involved – as you will gain confidence over time.

We do, however, try to produce some gardens that require less looking-after than others, and these often consist of a high proportion of grasses or evergreens, often mixed with interesting hard-landscaping materials. Hedges within a garden are pretty low-maintenance, as they usually require trimming only once a year, with some varieties needing to be trimmed twice. Generally, trees are easy to look after, as long as the right variety is picked for the location, as you don't want it to outgrow its location too quickly. Sometimes, however, we do increase the density of planting, as I often find that if there is less bare soil showing, you are less likely to get weed growth. This leads me on to the importance of mulching, which comes in many different styles. Mulching enables water retention, so the garden requires less irrigation, and at the same time it conceals the irrigation pipework. If geotextile is applied and then a layer of mulch, it will suppress the weeds as well as enhancing the identity of the garden.

I would think extremely carefully about having a lawn in any small garden, but if you do, make sure you lay a proper edge that will help with its maintenance, as lawns do require a lot of upkeep during the growing season. More often than not, small gardens are shady, so grass will not always do well and may take a long time to look good. Other types of planting may give you more pleasure and take less time to look after.

Many gardens have an area that needs to be low-maintenance, as it is not often used, such as a storage space where the dustbins (trash cans) are kept or the place where vehicles are parked, and often plants in containers are the best option for these spaces. Sometimes it's worth thinking outside the box, as we did when designing the garden of a Mediterranean holiday (vacation) home (left). The enclosed space had quite a dense canopy of pine trees, so very little else would grow. It had to be low-maintenance but still have impact, so we decided to lay strips of different-coloured gravels in wave shapes to represent water, as the property was near the coast.

In this courtyard (opposite top), we planted three rows of *Buxus sempervirens* in a bed edged with a *Buxus* hedge and with a *Phyllostachys nigra* on either side of the doorway. Planting rows of the same plant in multiples of three is one of my favourite devices. **In this minimal front garden (opposite below),** we planted three white-flowering cherries (*Prunus avium* 'Plena') with solid panels of *Buxus sempervirens* at their base. These are balanced by metal powder-coated containers planted with *Buxus* spheres. **This charming terraced Mediterranean garden (above)** really only needed the *Santolina chamaecyparissus* and lavenders cut back once a year to maintain them, making it reasonably low-maintenance and easy to care for (see also overleaf).

THE MEDITERRANEAN GARDEN

This is the garden of a superb boutique hotel in the most stunning location in Mougins in the South of France. When we helped the current owner to renovate it, the basic structure was intact, so we worked around the existing pathways, the canopy of trees and the large, old *Agave americana*.

We added some lovely, aged olive trees (*Olea europaea*) to underline the garden's authenticity. We also enlarged and reshaped the flowerbeds, and almost completely replanted the understorey. Over time, plants in Mediterranean gardens can become overgrown and woody, so it's often best to pull them out and start again, which is pretty much what we did. The garden was designed and planted in a linear way, but as the plants grew, its identity became softer, punctuated by the architectural *Agave americana*. We wanted to use a wider selection of plants to help give more colour throughout the year, and this was achieved by adding Bearded irises, both blue- and white-flowering *Agapanthus*, together with different varieties of lavender. We also added further interest with cream clay pots planted with lavender at every step junction where there were low pillars. Once planted and established, the beds were mulched with a locally sourced gravel, both to cover the irrigation pipes and to help suppress any weed growth. Apart from trimming the old lavender flowers and the *Santolina* flowers – I don't like their yellow flowers – this is a reasonably low-maintenance selection of plants and the mix of aromas in the sunshine is intoxicating.

These stone terraces (above) were a joy to replant. I love the way the *Agave americana* bursts forth from a mass of *Santolina chamaecyparissus* planted in parallel lines. I repeated this on the terrace behind, and the lovely domes of planting work well with the upright *Rosmarinus officinalis* and the gnarled olive.

The parallel lines of planting jump across the pathway. Using the same varieties strengthens the architectural identity of the planting.

The terracing needed something to anchor it, so we planted this lovely mature olive tree.

I wanted to emphasize the way to the hotel, so we added cream clay pots of lavender to every low pillar.

The edges of the flowerbeds were previously straight but I wanted to introduce curves to help bring a softer feel to the garden.

The clay pots of lavender (left) migrate through the garden, and their colour and texture complement the natural stone of the pathway and the various soft hues and textures within the foliage of the plants. The play of shadows in this garden (below) is magical, as we often get dappled sunlight filtering through the pines and olives, which brings out the heady mix of fragrance from the *Santolina*, *Helichrysum*, lavender, rosemary and thyme.

CONTAINER GARDENING

Gardening in containers can be rewarding, creative and inspirational. There are endless possibilities for putting together interesting combinations of plants to provide a natural backdrop for your outside space and to furnish it with colour, texture and fragrance. On one roof garden I designed (see overleaf), I essentially planted individual gardens in a series of oversized round pots made of white plastic.

When you are planting a balcony or small roof garden, you are often restricted to gardening in containers. Also, for various reasons, there may be an area in a garden – near the house, for example – where you are unable to plant in the ground, or there may be a paved or decked space that needs dressing, and often pots are just the right idea. Containers can be found in a wide variety of materials – including plastic, clay, wood and metal – to suit all styles of gardens, and they may be textured, smooth or coloured, depending on the look you are trying to create. Metal fabricated containers, which can be powder-coated in a wide choice of colours, making them very versatile, are one of my favourites.

Always use as large a pot as possible. People often use containers that are too small and then wonder why the plants don't do well, but if the pots are small, the plants will dry out quickly and become rooted through. Weight is always an issue on a roof garden or balcony, so do ask a surveyor to advise you.

Oxford planters filled with a mass of pink tulips (above left) look great on this decked roof garden with a line of three tall clay pots planted with spheres of *Buxus sempervirens*. Placed three in a row, my trademark tall galvanized pots with willow-weave covers (above right) tie in with the metal furniture. The zinc dish on a plinth (right), filled with burgundy and orange pansies, is flanked by low clay containers of *Helichrysum italicum*, *Scabiosa*, *Erysimum* 'Bowles's Mauve', *Salvia officinalis* 'Purpurascens' and *Lavandula angustifolia* 'Hidcote', for year-round interest. Three clay pots (opposite) are planted with different varieties of succulents: *Kalanchoe tomentosa* in the foreground, then *Kalanchoe beharensis* and *Echeveria* 'Pollux'.

CONTAINER KNOW-HOW

Use overscaled pots wherever you can as they always add a wow factor and a sense of drama. Large square zinc planters are firm favourites of mine. If weight is an issue, they can be half-filled with polystyrene and topped up with lightweight compost, as this won't affect the growth of herbaceous plants.

Introduce an unexpected element. One way to do this is by playing with scale – try planting tall, clear-stemmed *Magnolia grandiflora* in very tall, skinny terrazzo pots and underplanting them with seasonal colour.

Use containers to draw the eye and define space. For example, a line of pots can lead the eye along a path, divide one area from another, define a boundary or echo linear planting elsewhere in the garden.

The colour of your pots as well as what you plant in them is a contributory factor to your overall scheme. Choose your containers to tone in with other elements or to add bursts of accent colour.

Consider their shape, too. Tall, skinny containers will draw the eye upwards, creating height; large, broad pots necessarily take up more floor space.

Arrange containers either in pairs or odd numbers; three in a row makes the perfect statement.

Think about whether the style of container lends itself to additional detail, such as circular rings of neon lighting to tie in with the garden's colour scheme.

CASE STUDY
ROOF GARDEN

We designed this roof garden as if it were a drawing room with a dining table at one side. The seating area comprises two generous-sized sofas and a pair of armchairs, with a centrally placed coffee table, complete with its own firebowl, which lines up with a self-contained zinc water feature.

Both the coffee table and dining table are topped with the same Carrara marble that was used for the interior dining table and kitchen worktop. All the furniture is set on grey porcelain tiles, which were also used in the adjoining interior, softened by a dark grey exterior rug. A natural screen was created by placing eight oversized pots behind the glass balustrade, planted with *Eucalyptus gunnii*, *Betula utilis* var. *jacquemontii* and *Olea europaea*, with seasonal underplanting in different styles, to form individual gardens. One year we had an all-white spring colour scheme, whereas here we have a mix of pink and red tulips with white hyacinths. The white pots are lit by colour-changing LED lights and take on the colour of the light, completely changing the feel of the garden (see pages 48–9). A pair of uplights within each pot highlights the stems of the eucalyptus, silver birch or olive trees, creating a magical effect.

Behind the clear glass balustrade on two sides of the roof garden we placed a series of eight overscaled white pots, each planted as an individual garden.

The zinc water feature sits well on the grey porcelain tiles, creating a symphony of grey along with the dark grey exterior rug.

On either side of the central double doors are low zinc planters, planted seasonally, here with mixed tulips.

The white Carrara marble table matches the interior table and kitchen worktops.

Tulipa 'White Dream' (far left) is a firm favourite of mine, and one year we planted this garden with all-white spring bulbs. *Digitalis* (foxgloves) (centre left) grow well under *Betula utilis* var. *jacquemontii* for woodland-style container planting.

In the early summer, *Allium karataviense* **(left)** flowers alongside *Lavandula pedunculata* underneath the *Olea europaea* – Mediterranean-style planting.

The marble-topped coffee table (below), with its ethanol firebowl, acts as a central focal point that lines up with the self-contained zinc water feature, creating a vista to the *Olea europaea* planted centrally on both sides.

LIVING WALLS

A wave of this style of planting emerged around the beginning of the twenty-first century, with the French designer Patrick Blanc leading the way with his concept for planted walls. Over the years, we have been working with different styles of construction, some using pockets, pouches and troughs, which are planted and irrigated. Often the system can add a layer of insulation to a building, as we frequently apply them to façades of apartments, houses and light wells.

As technology keeps on advancing, our larger installations are monitored via a computer on a daily basis for watering and feeding, so an interesting range of plants can be used. On the lower part of the wall, we often have plants that will appreciate a shadier location, such as ferns, and as we go higher up, where it is sometimes sunnier, we tend to use plants that don't mind drier conditions.

I have found, over the years, that living walls are a very useful way of bringing life into locations where space is at a premium. They can create a magical effect in places where we are not able to plant directly into the ground, and so have proven to be a great way to create atmosphere in some rather difficult locations.

The walls of the smoking terrace at The Club at The Ivy in London (right) were inspired by a woven wooden fence. I had the walls fabricated so that every other section of the wavy façade was pulled out to form a planter, complete with built-in uplights, which were planted with a selection of ivy topiaries.
Various types of plants were used for this living wall (above), including *Vinca minor*, *Asplenium scolopendrium*, *Heuchera* 'Marmalade', *Polystichum tsussimense* and, for early spring colour, *Helleborus niger*.
The two slatted timber panels (opposite) cover the irrigation tanks and feeding filters, which are fully automated and regulated by daily computer readings. Three overscaled clay pots are planted with pleached *Carpinus betulus*, to form a 'hedge' on stilts for privacy.

CASE STUDY
VERTICAL GARDEN

Living walls brighten up any dull area in a garden where space is at a premium. Choose plants according to the amount of light available – sunny locations allow you a wider selection, while ferns are the best choice for shady or damp spaces, such as this courtyard within a small urban garden. It seemed the perfect choice to bring greenery up from the basement to the top of the fencing at the first-floor level.

We edged the living wall with a timber surround, with a slatted timber cover to hide the irrigation equipment, and we used lovely, solid pieces of timber to create the staircase up to the conservatory, which looked down onto this compact garden. As the surrounding walls were very tall, we clad them in open square trellis and planted lots of fragrant *Trachelospermum*, which produced a heady fragrance all summer long. In the top right-hand corner of the garden we planted a cloud-pruned olive, and in the opposite corner a cloud-pruned holly (*Ilex crenata*). A stone sculpture was positioned as a focal point at the end of the vista as you enter the garden from the lower-ground-floor kitchen (see page 117). The garden is furnished with a large slatted exterior sofa and a coffee table, placed on our trademark panel of timber decking, representing an exterior rug, within the grey stone paving. We ran an LED light along the underside of the sofa, to provide a glow of light underneath it at night. There are also a pair of occasional chairs and a small round table in front of the set of three clay pots within the top bed planting. My favourite part of this garden is the clear glass walkway over the light well below, which looks really magical at night.

The wonderful view (opposite) looks up through the clear glass walk-over panel from the basement light well, which is uplit at night. **This three-storey living wall (below)** starts in the basement and continues past the clear glass walkway at the lower ground floor and up to the top of the neighbour's fence at ground level. Although it is only 1.2m (4ft) wide, it creates a dramatic statement that connects the whole house together.

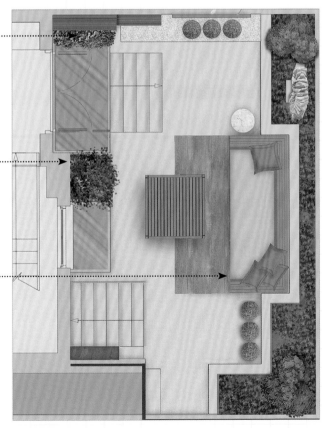

The living wall is encased in a slatted timber surround, which also covers the irrigation and feeding equipment.

A metal powder-coated container is used here to enable climbers to cover the back of the house.

The exterior sofa has an LED light strip on its underside, which gives a warm, atmospheric glow to the garden.

PLANTING

LINEAR PLANTING

I have introduced the idea of linear planting into many of our garden design projects over the past five or six years, and it has become one of our signature statements. However, it is nothing new. I was inspired by the bulb fields in Holland, where they have been cultivating bulbs for hundreds of years in this way.

The spectacular bulb planting that I admired in Holland, with rows and rows of different-coloured tulips stretching as far as the eye can see, inspired me to use this linear planting technique with native plants, which gives a very architectural appearance straight after planting. As some varieties of plants grow, the lines soften and change, so it is fascinating to see how the effect transforms throughout the seasons and as the plants mature. In countries where seasonality is a factor, I also like to mix evergreens into my plant selection, as they add another dimension to the planting.

I love repetition in gardens, as it creates a strong impact, even in the smallest of spaces. Multiple lines of the same variety of plant can almost seem like an art installation. Always use a minimum of three plants in a row and try to work in multiples of odd numbers – five, seven, nine, for example – because this is more pleasing to the eye.

When making your selection, be mindful of how different plants grow and their habit. The scale of the plants you are intending to use is also an important consideration. Although the process can be quite complex, it is exciting to explore different ideas and try out new combinations. As with any plant selection, it is great to work with different leaf forms, textures and colours, as well as combining plants that flower at different times of the year.

When planning your linear planting, it's often a good idea to leave the odd line out, so that you have the flexibility to add seasonal colour – be that spring- or summer-flowering bulbs, or summer bedding. Sometimes I plant lines of *Elaeagnus* x *ebbingei* within a scheme, which can be grown into formal clipped hedges to help divide up a garden.

Agave americana (top left) look architectural against lines of orange Bearded iris, chosen to link in with the Corten steel edging of the adjacent driveway. **Linear seasonal bulb planting (top right),** as often seen in Holland. *Tulipa* 'Fontainebleau' works well with the red brick of the house, while *Tulipa* 'Dordogne' tones with the gravel paths. **Lines of Mediterranean-style plants (above left)** include *Lavandula stoechas, Teucrium fruticans, Agave americana* and *Gaura lindheimeri,* which has billowing flowers all summer. ***Hosta*** 'Halcyon' (above right) works well with *Polystichum setiferum,* next to rows of *Uncinia rubra* and *Iris* 'Kent Pride'.

The hedge of dark green yew (*Taxus baccata*) (left) divides the dining terrace from the linear garden, which features rows of *Tulipa* 'Queen of Night', planted between *Aquilegia vulgaris* var. *stellata* 'Black Barlow' and *Tulipa* 'Menton', next to *Teucrium fruticans*, with its lovely silvery grey foliage. This ties in well with the grey metal frames of the windows and the architectural detail on the back of this property, while the black tulips pick up on the black granite kitchen worktops, which 'float' through the glass on the ground floor. On either side of the exterior barbecue grill are huge, clear glass vases, which we filled with water to submerge long stems of tulips, some upside down. Uplit from below, the glass magnifies the flowers to create magical arrangements.

PLANTING

183

CASE STUDY
PERFECTLY BALANCED

This Mediterranean garden has a great feeling of space due to the fact that we have used a limited palette of plants. Lovely old *Olea europaea* are planted quite closely together at each end of the plot to help blur the boundaries; it seems as if they have been there some time, giving the garden an authentic and established feel. Their trunks are set against the natural stone wall and contrast well with it. The repetition of the linear planting under the olive trees, using the same variety of plants right across the garden, creates a great feeling of depth.

The planting in the central part of this garden is quite low, with a large area of grass to balance out the expanse of the swimming pool beyond (see overleaf). When designing this garden, we took the main pathway as a central line, and you will notice that the planting on each side of the path is a mirror image of the other. This is a great device to adopt in small gardens, as it can make a space seem a lot larger than it really is. Each area of the house has its own section of decking under its individual concrete canopy. This relates well to the linear planting that surrounds the house, but as the lines also run the whole length of the garden, it not only works well close up but also creates a dramatic effect on a larger scale.

If you can design a swimming pool so that it looks like a reflective pool within a garden, as we did here, it looks even more magical. The reflective qualities alone are quite amazing, but it also sits very comfortably within its surroundings, making it a very relaxing space at all times of the day and especially at sunset, when it takes on another character altogether.

The lines of planting (opposite top left and right), featuring *Agave americana*, *Lavandula stoechas*, *Teucrium fruticans* and *Gaura lindheimeri* show up well against the natural stone walls. The beds are mulched with gravel from the same stone, which also conceals the irrigation pipes, so the landscape blends and the colours harmonize.

Whenever I am in this garden (opposite below), I can't help but marvel at the lines of planting, which take the eye out to sea, and I love the way the grey foliage of the plants mimics the ever-changing shades of the water beyond. The natural beauty of the landscape never ceases to amaze me and it's something mankind can't even begin to compete with – and neither should we try.

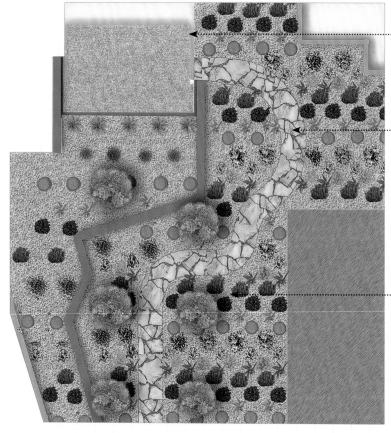

The landscape is taken up onto the roof of a room that looks out to sea.

The natural stone path meanders through the old olive trees to the entrance to this room in a very naturalistic way.

The linear planting continues for the entire length of the garden, jumping over the lawn and paths. The planting is mirrored on each side of the pathway.

184

Echinocactus grusonii (top right) is one of my favourite cactuses, as I love its architectural identity. Don't be fooled, though, when looking down into its fluffy centre – it's still very prickly.

The backdrop to this lovely flowerbed (below right) is a hedge of *Elaeagnus* x *ebbingei*, which I tend to use a lot in our Mediterranean gardens – I love its winter flowers with their intoxicating fragrance. Together with the amazing burgundy flowers of the *Melianthus major*, it works really well with the red freesias, which I often grow so they can be picked for the house.

The pool terrace (below) enjoys an uninterrupted view out to sea. I love the way certain varieties of plants tend to grow into mounds or clumps, as have the *Pittosporum tobira* 'Nanum' and *Santolina chamaecyparissus* in the planting bed alongside, while the *Teucrium fruticans* has been trimmed into shape.

I planted a series of spaces in between the walls separating the rooms (opposite) with neat lines of *Echinocactus grusonii* – there are 52 in total. As they can grow up to 1m (3ft) in diameter, I have left plenty of room in between them for growth. The effect is almost like a growing art installation, and I love the way they take your eye to the old, gnarled olive tree.

RESOURCES

SURFACES
Bex Blacksmith
Wild Fields Farm, Wood Street
Village, Guildford, GU3 3BP, UK
+44 (0)1483 828 898
www.bexsimon.com
Artist blacksmith

Biotecture Ltd
The Old Dairy, Ham Farm,
Main Road, Bosham, West Sussex,
PO18 8EH, UK
+44 (0)1243 572 118
www.biotecture.uk.com
Living walls

DG Glass Designs Ltd
Unit 13, IO Centre, 57 Croydon Road,
Croydon, Surrey, CR0 4WQ, UK
+44 (0)20 8090 6081
www.dgglassdesigns.co.uk
Glass

Easigrass
Easigrass Distribution Ltd
The Old Grass Depot, Park Avenue,
London, UB1 3AJ, UK
+44 (0)8450 948 880
www.easigrass.com
Artificial grass

The Garden Trellis Company
355A Old Road, Clacton-on-Sea,
Essex, CO15 3RQ, UK
+44 (0)1255 688 361
www.gardentrellis.co.uk
Trellis and other timber
garden structures

London Stone
8 Chertsey Road, Chobham,
Surrey, GU24 8NB, UK
+44 (0)8442 251 915
www.londonstone.co.uk
Natural stone paving

Natural Stone Projects
+44 (0)20 8943 3221
www.stone-projects.com
Natural stone products

LANDSCAPE CONTRACTORS
Landform Consultants
The Nursery, Bagshot Road,
Chobham, Surrey, GU24 8DB, UK
+44 (0)1276 856 145
www.landformconsultants.co.uk

Morgan Oates Ltd
6 Edensor Road, Chiswick,
London, W4 2RG, UK
+44 (0)20 8987 9470
www.morganoates.co

POTS, CONTAINERS & WATER FEATURES
Andrew Ewing
16 Talina Centre, 23a Bagleys Lane,
London, SW6 2BW, UK
+44 (0)20 7731 2757
www.andrewewing.co.uk
Water features

Atelier Vierkant
Sint-Jorisstraat 88a, B-8730
Beernem, Belgium
+32 50 370 056
www.ateliervierkant.be
Clay pots

Domani
Vlaamse Kaai 35, 2000 Antwerp,
Belgium
+32 3 291 44 60
www.domani.be
Pots, containers and water features

Whichford Pottery
Whichford, Nr Shipston on Stour,
Warwickshire, CV36 5PG, UK
+44 (0)1608 684416
www.whichfordpottery.com
Pots

GARDEN FURNITURE
Brown Jordan
20 Kingbrook Parkway,
Simpsonville, KY 40067, USA
bjccustomerservice@brownjordan.com
www.brownjordan.com

Gaze Burvill (UK)
Lodge Farm, East Tisted,
Hampshire, GU34 3QH, UK
+44 (0)1420 588 444
www.gazeburvill.com

Gaze Burvill (USA)
+1 (917) 691 6187

Gaze Burvill (Germany)
+49 (0)6723 673 3715

Gloster furniture
Gloster Furniture Limited, Bristol, UK
+44 (0)1454 631 950
www.gloster.com

Holly Hunt (USA)
979 Third Avenue, Suite 503/605,
New York, NY 10022, USA
+1 (0)212 755 6555
www.hollyhunt.com

Holly Hunt (UK)
20 Grafton Street, London,
W1S 4DZ, UK
+44 (0)20 7399 3280

McKinnon and Harris (USA)
1806 Summit Avenue, Richmond,
VA 23230, USA
+1 804 358 2385
www.mckinnonharris.com

McKinnon and Harris (UK)
220 North Dome, Design Centre,
Chelsea Harbour, London,
SW10 0XE, UK
+44 (0)20 7349 9085

Roda
Roda Srl, Via Tinella, 2, 21026
Gavirate – VA, Italy
+39 0332 74 86
www.rodaonline.com

Sutherland
68 Regal Row, Dallas, TX 75247, USA
+1 214 638 4161
www.sutherlandfurniture.com

LIGHTING
Breathe Lighting
7 Ullenwood Court, Ullenwood,
Cheltenham, Gloucestershire,
GL53 9QS, UK
+44 (0)8452 636 333
www.breathelighting.co.uk

Collingwood (UK)
Brooklands House, Sywell Aerodrome,
Sywell, Northants, NN6 0BT, UK
+44 (0)1604 495 151
www.collingwoodlighting.com

Collingwood (France)
+33 (0)4 816 816 10

Collingwood (Germany)
+49 (0)8941 112 3777

Design Plus Light
K210 – The Biscuit Factory,
100 Clements Road, London,
SE16 4DG, UK
+44 (0)20 8762 9585
www.designpluslight.com

Hunza (Worldwide)
www.hunza.co.nz

Hunza (UK)
Heath House, Bewdley Business
Park, Long Bank, Bewdley,
Worcestershire, DY12 2TZ, UK
+44 (0)1299 269 950
www.lightideas.co.uk

Light IQ
1 Rylett Studios, 77 Rylett Crescent,
London, W12 9RP, UK
+44 (0)20 8749 1900
www.lightiq.com

OUTDOOR FIREPLACES
Urban Fires
186–192 Sutton Court Road, London,
W4 3HR, UK
+44 (0)20 7183 1806
www.urbanfires.co.uk

KITCHENS & BARBECUES
Big Green Egg
Alfresco Concepts Ltd, The Ropley,
The Dene, Ropley, Alresford,
Hampshire, SO24 0BG, UK
+44 (0)8432 162 805
www.biggreenegg.com
Barbecues

McCarron Kitchens
Clackersbrook Farm,
46 The Common, Bromham,
Wiltshire, SN15 2JJ, UK
+44 (0)1380 859299
www.mccarronandco.com
Kitchen specialist

AWNINGS
Indigo Awnings
The Barn, Bryn Bellan, Bryn Road,
Mold, CH7 5DE, UK
+44 (0)8450 508 969
www.indigoawnings.co.uk

PLANTS & GARDEN SUPPLIES
Crocus
Nursery Court, London Road,
Windlesham, Surrey, GU20 6LQ, UK
+44 (0)1344 578 000
Orders: (0)1344 578 111
www.crocus.co.uk

Deepdale Trees Ltd
Tithe Farm, Hatley Road, Potton
Sandy, Bedfordshire, SG19 2DX, UK
+44 (0)1767 262 636
www.deepdale-trees.co.uk
Specimen trees and shrubs

DeJager Bulbs
Church Farm, Ulcombe, Maidstone,
Kent, ME17 1DN, UK
+44 (0)1622 840 229
www.dejager.co.uk
Dutch bulbs

Europlants UK Ltd
Great North Road, Bell Bar, Hatfield,
Hertfordshire, AL9 6DA, UK
+44 (0)1707 649 996
www.europlants.net
Plant supply (wholesale)

INDEX
Figures in italics refer to captions.

PICTURE CREDITS

The author and publisher would like to thank the following photographers and companies for their kind permission to reproduce the photographs in this book.

© **Stephen Woodhams:** pages 1, 7 above left; 7 above right, 7 below left, 8–9, 11 right, 12, 13, 14, 15, 16, 17 above left, 18, 22, 23, 24, 25, 26, 32 above right, 32 below left, 32 below right, 33, 36, 37, 38, 42 above, 44, 47 above, 52–3, 55, 56 centre, 58–9, 61, 62, 63, 64, 66 above right, 66 below right, 67 above, 68 left, 69, 71 below, 72 centre, 72–3, 76, 77, 78 left, 82, 83, 84, 85 above, 86, 88, 89 below, 90, 91 below, 92 left, 94 above, 97 above left, 97 below left, 98, 99, 100–1, 101 above right, 102–3, 104 above, 104 below left, 105, 106–7, 108 left, 108–9, 110 below, 111 below, 111 above right, 112 above, 116 above right, 116 below left, 118 above right, 118 below right, 119, 120–1, 122, 123, 124, 125 above, 126–7, 128, 129 below, 130, 132 above right, 133, 134, 135, 136, 137, 139 above right, 140 above, 141 right, 142–3, 145, 146 above left, 146 above right, 146 below left, 150, 151, 152, 153, 154, 155, 156 below, 157 above centre right, 157 above right, 157 below, 158, 159 above left, 159 above centre left, 159 above centre right, 161 right, 164–5, 165 right, 166, 167, 168, 169 below, 170, 171, 172, 173, 174, 175, 176, 176–7, 177, 178 below, 181 left, 182 above left, 182 above right, 182 below left, 184, 185 above right.

© **Heiner Orth:** pages 2, 4–5, 10–11, 17 below right, 19, 20, 21, 27, 28, 29, 30, 31, 39, 40, 41, 43 above right, 50–1, 56 left, 57, 60–1, 65, 66 above left, 70, 71 above, 74–5, 78–9, 80, 81, 87, 89 above, 92–3, 94 below, 95, 96–7, 97 above right, 97 below right, 101 above left, 104 below right, 111 centre right, 116 centre right, 132 bottom left, 132 bottom right, 139 bottom right, 144, 146 below right, 147, 156 above, 183, 185 above left, 185 below, 186 above, 187.

© **Clive Nichols:** page 7 below right, 32 above left, 34–5, 35, 43 above left, 43 below, 46, 50 above right, 51 above, 54, 67 below, 68 right, 91 above, 110 131 below above, 111 above left, 117, 118 above left, 159 above right, 160 above, 169 above centre left, 169 above centre right, 169 above left, 178 above, 180, 181 right.

© **Mike Toy:** page 42 below, 66 below left.

© **Sabine Weismann:** page 45, 47 below, 140 below.

© **Bernard Viljoen:** page 48–9, 141 left, 157 above left, 157 above centre left, 169 above right, 182 below right.

© **Nina Campbell:** page 72 left.

© **Elizabeth Terry:** page 111 centre left, 112 below, 113, 114–15, 125 below, 159 below.

© **Jürgen Becker:** page 129 above, 148–9, 186 centre, 186 below.

© **Thomas Griem:** page 131 above, 139 above left.

© **Gaze Burvill:** page 139 bottom left.

© **Gary Rogers:** pages 160–1, 162–3.

© **James Merrell:** page 179.

Courtesy of Hunza: page 50 above left, 50 centre left below, 50 below left, 56 above right, 56 centre right below, 56 below right.

Courtesy of Collingwood: page 50 centre left above, 56 centre right above.

Courtesy of Springfields: page 85 below.

Courtesy of Roda: page 138 centre above, 138 centre below, 138 above left, 138 above right.

Courtesy of Sutherland: page 138 bottom left.

Every effort has been made to trace the copyright holders. We apologize in advance for any unintentional omissions and would be pleased to insert the appropriate acknowledgement in any subsequent editions.

ACKNOWLEDGEMENTS

I have many people to thank for helping me with this book. First and foremost, my partner Salim Esmail, whose love, support, patience and guidance have been much appreciated.

To Keith Pocock, for all his help and support over the past few years, and for keeping us laughing and on track at the office, even under times of pressure.

To all my clients, who have so kindly allowed me to photograph their gardens and make this book possible.

To Jacqui Small, who I have enjoyed working with again, 21 years after we published my first book together. To my art director and designer, Manisha Patel, and my editors, Zia Mattocks, Eszter Karpati and Emma Heyworth-Dunn, and to the photographers, Heiner Orth, Clive Nichols, Gary Rogers, Jürgen Becker.

Then, in no particular order, to Sabine Weismann, Colin Livingston, Josh for laying the turf shown on the endpapers, Dan Oates, Matt Sears and his brilliant photo, Barbara Samatier, Dan McCarthey, Camilla Richards, Denise O'Donoghue, Brent and Genevieve Hoberman, Thomas and Eve Henderson, Michael Spencer, Rhona Lubner, Susie Beart, Joanna Wood, Charles Dunstone, Barbara Wilby, Paul Jones, Anna and Mike Penn, Lux* Belle Mare, Tom and Kuljit Singh, Susan Sangster, Tony Hilliard, Barbara Sulzberger, Michael and Brigitta Freund, Mark Abbott and Irfan Ghani, Charles Worthington and Allan Peters, Marina and Francesco Moncada, Nina Campbell, Ian and Sarah Burton, David and Annie Guest, Nick and Annette Mason, Angie O'Rourke, Mary and Jeffrey Archer, Alison Prince, Barnsley House Hotel, Stephen Teale, Andrew Garnet and Daren Wallace, Springfields Shopping Centre, Tom Speechley, Smallbone, Mark Brook and Stephen Ryan, Lorraine Spencer, Jasmine Al Fayed, Elizabeth and Ian Terry – with a special mention to Elizabeth for her lovely pictures – Yasmin Karim, Tom Stogdon, Mary Fox-Linton, Gail and Gerald Ronson, Nils Wager, Thomas and Lili Griem, Sanjit Bahra, Stephen Roper, Gaze Burvill, Christopher and Anne Evans, Lyn Finch, The Swan at Lavenham, Merrill Lynch, The Ivy Club, Henry Moore Court, William Yeoward and Colin Orchard, Jaime Romano, Renato Canale, Andreu Crespi, Angie Diggle and Peter Romaniuk.